The Art of
Auditioning

TECHNIQUES FOR
TELEVISION

Rob Deci

ALLWORTH PRESS
NEW YORK

08 07 06 05 04   5 4 3 2 1

Published by Allworth Press
An imprint of Allworth Communications, Inc.
10 East 23rd Street, New York, NY 10010

Cover design by Derek Bacchus
Page composition/typography by Integra

ISBN: 1-58115-353-8

LIBRARY OF CONGRESS CATALOGING-IN-PUBLICATION DATA

Decina, Rob.
    The art of auditioning: techniques for television/by Rob Decina.
        p.   cm.
Includes bibliographical references and index.
ISBN 1-58115-353-8 (pbk.)
1. Television acting.   2. Acting—Auditions.   3. Television broadcasting—Auditions.   I. Title.

PN1992.8.A3D43 2004
791.4502'8—dc22

                                              2004004433

Printed in Canada

For Jen, and Kayley, and Aidan.

This book is also dedicated to every teacher
I ever had who told me I didn't
have the attention span to even read a book—
well, now I wrote one.

Table of Contents

Acknowledgments

I would like to thank all of the people in the industry who had enough confidence in me to give me an opportunity to be a casting director. Among those people are Mark Saks, the late Barbara Miller, Paul Rauch, John Conboy, Ellen Wheeler, and Mickey Dwyer-Dobbin. I would also like to thank everyone at *Guiding Light* who was so supportive when I was writing this book, most notably the casting staff of Melanie Haseltine-Master and Darlene Failla.

I would also like to thank all of the casting directors, agents, and actors whose input, advice, and friendship over the years have greatly added to this book.

I would like to thank all of my teachers for allowing me to understand what they know about the art of theatre and the craft of acting, including Paul Austin, John McCormack, and Ruis Woertendyke, to name just a few.

I would also like to thank all the people who have allowed me to teach, including Bob Klaeger, Shirley Kaplan, Dennis Reid, Arielle Tepper, Beth Wicke, and Alan Nusbaum.

In addition, I would also like to thank my entire family, especially my parents who have always supported my endeavors, and my wife Jennifer, who always encourages me to believe in myself.

In addition, I would also like to thank my entire family, especially my parents, for, among other things, going to every single theatre production I was ever involved in.

Last, I would like to thank everyone at Allworth Press for supporting and believing in this book and technique, including Nicole Potter, Michael Madole, Jessica Rozler, and Tad Crawford.

A special thanks to Bill Runyon, whose courage and humor inspire me.

Introduction

I am writing this book with the idea of helping the beginning- to intermediate-level auditioner. However, those auditioners who have been pursuing a career for some time, but have failed to make any headway, may also pick up a new technique or benefit from a change in their approach to auditioning, based on what they read in this book. Notice I said *auditioner* and not *actor*. There is an important difference in those two titles; I will discuss that in the following chapters.

I am not suggesting this book for the young actor who is starting his or her training. A scene study or acting class will best serve those actors. This book is designed to help actors with their individual audition preparation as well as their actual "in-the-room" audition. If you are in a bookstore browsing the audition books section and have picked this book up, you probably could benefit from it. If you are starting to meet casting directors, or have just signed with an agent, this book will help you. If you are just out of college, a theatre program, or a conservatory, you could use this book to help you in your transition from theatrical training to audition training. You don't need this book if you have ever tested, or ever landed a role in a television pilot or a daytime television series. Something is working for you, and you should stick with it. However, by all means, feel free to purchase and read.

I have also written this book as a companion for any workshop class that I teach. Often I feel that I am verbalizing more information than can be absorbed, and the idea of having it in print seems helpful to those students/actors, and to me, as a teaching tool.

When I became a full-time, full-fledged casting director, I made a startling discovery. I realized that the audition process is somewhat of a mystery to most actors. Truth be told, it was a mystery to me too. Auditioning is a job interview for actors. It is a job interview that has inherent restrictions and limitations. Working within those limitations is the key to a successful first audition. That is what this book will cover: the limitations, the challenges, the choices, and the mistakes that actors and casting directors make—all the factors that no one talks about, that no one teaches.

This book will discuss my "philosophy" of auditioning as well as a practical and challenging audition technique. I will explain in detail my specific audition technique—one that I feel is helpful for actors looking to get ahead and stand out. This will be the heart of the book. I will be honest and direct while describing the traps that both actors and casting directors fall into. My hope is that this book will empower the actor and help guide him or her from the first meeting/audition to the callback and through the screen test process. The technique's focus is the television audition, but I am confident it can be used for the film audition as well.

Before I go any further, let me preface all this by saying that I am not the best casting director or teacher in the industry. There are people who have more experience. However, what I do have is a real love for the craft of acting. I understand and appreciate it and feel confident that I understand actors as well. I appreciate actors and have great respect for their ambitions. Before becoming a casting director, I was a theatre director, paying my dues in New York City. When I was an undergraduate communications student at Pace University, I dabbled in the college theatre program. My professor, Dr. Ruis Woertendyke, encouraged me to study and learn about the craft of acting. He thought directing came naturally to me, and suggested I sharpen my skills in graduate school. I listened, and I have been appreciative of his advice ever since. I attended Sarah Lawrence College, where I received my Master of Fine Arts degree in Theatre.

It is there that I began to understand the craft of acting as an art form and as a skill that must be worked on. While in graduate school, I did a semester-long internship at a film casting office. That is where I first had the opportunity to witness actors in this unique thing we call "auditioning." After graduating, I pursued theatre by accepting internships and assistant director positions at such places as the Berkshire Theatre Festival, the Juilliard School of Drama, and the Manhattan Theatre Club, to name a few, and began working with some of the best directors, playwrights, and actors in the community. I also began working with young playwrights, developing plays and directing staged readings. I was directing, both Off-Off Broadway and at young, new theatre companies throughout the New York region. Soon I started teaching where I could and began coaching actors with their monologue auditions. While I was juggling all this and pounding the pavement as a young director, I was fortunate enough to acquire freelance work as a casting assistant with a top film casting director. This allowed me to enhance my casting resume as I pursued my directing career and to be involved in the audition process with many recognizable faces. Shortly after that, I received a full-time job offer to be a casting assistant at Warner Bros. Television in New York. This was a turning point in my own career, because it indicated a commitment to the world of casting. This was one of the busiest television casting offices in New York. I was able to immerse myself in the world of primetime television casting, learning under one of the best television casting directors. Within a year, I was promoted to an associate casting director; a year later, I left that position to become the casting director for *Guiding Light*.

I tell you all this so you can see how I got to where I am. It is also important to me that you recognize the varied background I have in both the art of theatre and the business of film and television. This book combines what I have been taught with my insight into and interpretation of what I have observed and experienced. I have had some of the best teachers in my own education, and have worked with some of the best casting directors, producers, and directors in the television industry. The technique that I have developed is designed to help actors succeed in the television medium. Please read with an open mind. Please keep in mind that I am one casting director, one teacher with my own opinions. My opinions may greatly differ from those of my peers. What is important is that you trust what I am saying and give it a practical application in the real world. If it doesn't work for you, fine; if it does work for you, even better. Perhaps only a portion of the technique will be applicable for you, while, for others, the entire technique may be accessible.

I am writing this book as a source of encouragement. I love actors. I want actors to succeed. As a casting director, I *need* actors to succeed. You are the solution to my daily challenge of casting roles (getting actors jobs). That's what this book is about: how to book the job. Keeping that job is another book!

CHAPTER 1

Auditioning and the Craft of Acting

Auditioning and acting are two different things. Here's the truth: A great actor does not make a great auditioner. An actor who can audition well is not necessarily a good actor. Can you be great at auditioning and be an interesting actor? Of course—this is what you should be striving for. But remember, you are trying to *book the job* in the audition, and that's what we will focus on here.

Acting is a Craft

Acting is a craft—one that must be studied, practiced, and developed. It is an ongoing process of learning and maturing. I believe that the actor who understands the craft is better prepared to audition than the actor who is only looking to become famous and doesn't take the craft seriously.

A first audition is an opportunity to display your potential in a role, to show how you might play that character if given the opportunity to apply your craft. So, the audition becomes about an actor's approach to applying craft within the limitations of an audition. Audition technique does not take as long to master as the craft itself, but my philosophy begins with the belief that you must appreciate the craft to develop the audition skills. Most importantly, you must understand that they are indeed separate skills.

So, you must study the craft of acting before you can approach the art of auditioning. The craft is what you will rely on in your career and in the day-to-day challenges that an actor will face on a job. The audition is a display of that craft. It is where the craft and the business of trying to get an acting job on television meet. If you are reading this book and you have yet to begin your journey into studying and understanding the craft, I urge you to consider taking classes first. You can read this book, apply technique, and perhaps even book a job, but you will eventually need the craft of acting to get you through the challenges on the set, with a script, and in the work you do with other actors, directors, and producers. If you do not have the proper background, you will be faking it. You can fake it for a while, but not forever. There are no shortcuts to a sustained career.

So, read the books by the great teachers and study at the best schools. Get yourself ready for an incredible journey into learning the skills of acting. Then, take those skills and learn a technique that will allow you to display aspects of your skills for a specific role in a given opportunity. That opportunity will be your audition.

CHAPTER 2

An Audition is Not a Performance

An audition is not a performance. It is not a mini-performance, either. A performance is the furthest thing from what an audition should be. It is also not a scene or a workshop opportunity. It is not class. It is a business interview where actors are going to be evaluated for their acting talent and their appropriateness for a given character.

In my opinion, most actors come to an audition with the idea that they have to put on a performance. This is not the best approach, because it is nearly impossible to accomplish. The key to auditioning is to *show potential*. The way you show potential is by setting up realistic and obtainable goals. You must recognize the limitations inherent in a first audition for a role, then set your goals accordingly.

Let's look at this. The first time I audition an actor for any given role, I am in my office. That's right, an office. I sit at my desk, my computer is there, the track lighting is on, and I have no windows. For the record, the walls are painted a mystic gray. Here's my point: It's an office! It is not a theatre. It is not a stage. It is not even a sound stage or a set. It is what it is. You can't change that. I would say that 90 percent of the time I am playing the part of the reader for the actors who are auditioning. That means I am sitting in my chair, behind my desk, reading with the actor and evaluating at the same time. If the actor's expectations are for a performance, I cannot meet him halfway. I cannot collaborate on choices or ideas. I don't have time, and I also don't want to.

The same is true when I am just observing. My assistant or associate will usually be the reader when I am not. They are good, but they are not actors, and they are instructed not to act or make choices, but rather just to give the actors something to play off of. Sometimes they get the material moments before they sit in their chair. If you are prepared to give a performance, you will expect too much from the reader. A scene needs two actors with choices, objectives, and feelings. This isn't a scene; it's an audition.

A theatrical presentation cannot be fulfilled within the limitations of an office and an audition. Even one's preparation should be different. Theatrical preparation such as sense memory work and coming in "as character" is wasted energy in an audition. If this were a theatre audition, it would be different, but we are talking about television. Many times in television you do not get a full script to read, so you're not able to get a sense of the life of the character. You may only have three to five pages. In theatre, you can usually get the full play. If you were showing two contrasting monologues for a regional theatre contract, acting methods would probably be appropriate for that venue.

I am not being disrespectful to television. I love television and my job. I am just being realistic as to what is required to succeed and gain attention. In the theatre, when you read a play, you can gain an understanding of the character's whole journey, and you can use this information to inform your interpretation of the character. In television, the writers will often make changes to the character's journey as the episodes go on. If you try to present a full interpretation of a character in a television audition, you're being too ambitious.

Choose Obtainable Goals

You must make choices that serve the audition sides, but that are still suitable to the environment. For example, if the scene calls for the characters to embrace, you must figure out a way to *emotionally* achieve the intent of that moment rather than actually achieve the *physical* moment. I am not going to get up for the embrace, and I shouldn't. If you have prepared the audition with the hope of the embrace taking place, then you will be thrown off when the reader does not do that.

The same rule applies for the use of props and blocking. I feel like the introduction of those elements is an effort to make the audition a production. This will be covered in detail in a later chapter.

For the same reason, I do not feel like you should be "off book" for a first audition. I expect the actor to have the sides in his hands to refer to during the audition. I actually prefer that to complete memorization. When the actor has his sides in his hands, it symbolically reminds us that this is an audition and not a performance. Also, I am much more interested in the actor's choices than his or her memorization skill. Some actors are very good at this, and I have had some insist it is the only way for them to audition, and that is fine. However, if those actors forget their lines during the audition, it has a negative effect on their evaluation. I have found that many young actors come to an audition with the scene memorized, only to struggle with remembering their lines once the actual audition begins. It would have been more impressive to me to see their choices rather than their memorization skills, or lack thereof.

Auditioning and Performing Are Two Different Things

This next part is important. You must acknowledge that the way you actually audition for a role is not necessarily the way you would perform the role, if you were lucky enough to book the role. If you can understand that concept, then you must bear that in mind as you prepare for the audition. Don't think in terms of a finished polished product. Don't visualize yourself doing the audition scene on a set. Visualize yourself doing it in a casting office.

When you are preparing for your audition, you must work very hard at doing the simple things well. I am sure you all have heard the advice that you must make big, interesting choices to stand out in an audition. That is not necessarily true. Most actors are so interested in making those big choices that they do not concentrate on the simple things. They do not ask themselves the simple and important questions: What does the character want? Does the character achieve what the character wants? How does the character feel? At the basic level, what I am looking for is thinking, feeling, living, and breathing beings. Characters who display passion and ambition. I am not concerned about props, wardrobe, blocking, or some deep level of character exploration. When you move forward in the process to a callback or screen test, you can start introducing more elaborate and performance-oriented choices. You can concentrate on the development of the character when you have the time to do so. The time allotted for the preparation of a first audition does not allow for the development of character. It barely allows for time to prepare for the audition itself. So, the first audition should be about showing potential.

When you book the job you will have a scene partner, with whom you will have rehearsal time to collaborate on choices. You will also be doing it with a director, on a set, with lights and cameras and hair and makeup people. That is when a performance is required and when those advanced choices can be fulfilled. Let's get the job before we perform the job.

CHAPTER 3

Audition Philosophy

Okay. Here's my thinking, my audition philosophy. It is very simple. As actors, you must accept the fact that you are *not* going to book the job that you are auditioning for. Your actual chances of getting that particular role are slim to none. Now, I am not trying to set up a defeatist attitude, but rather a realistic one. What I would really like to accomplish with this philosophy is to help you avoid expectations for positive results and feedback.

Actors put too much pressure on themselves when auditioning. Is this the audition that changes your life? Is this the role that will allow you to quit your restaurant job? Leave your temp job? Is this the role that will make you famous? Those pressures and anxieties are all negative influences on an actor. These pressures create an aura that is readable in the audition room. Negative elements create negative auditions. When a positive result is not accomplished, actors get down on themselves and take it personally. I am suggesting that you learn to free yourself from those overly hopeful expectations that result in negative feelings and face the inevitable: that you are not going to book this job. That information, that knowledge, is powerful for you. To clarify, I am referring to the lead roles on television shows; the series regular roles on a primetime series and the contract roles in daytime television. I am not discussing the smaller roles in those productions, for which there is less competition. I want you to focus on the big roles for now.

Truth in Numbers

The basis for this philosophy is rooted in a numbers game. Here is some reality for you to better understand my thinking. When I have a contract role to fill on *Guiding Light*, I personally audition between three hundred and five hundred actors for that role. As many as five hundred! Only one actor can actually book that job—just one. What are the odds that you will be the one actor out of the five hundred that auditions to actually get the job? What are the odds that you are physically what I am looking for and that on the day you audition your audition will be at the top of your game?

As I mentioned above, those odds are very slim. Here are some more numbers to think about. Out of the five hundred actors who have a first audition (sometimes called a "pre-screen"), only about twenty-five actors will get a producer callback for that role. Those are the twenty-five I feel best represent what we are looking for in that role. Twenty-five out of five hundred make it to the next round of the competition. Out of the twenty-five, only eight to twelve will be asked to screen test for the role, and, as you know, only one gets the role.

Now that is just a small example of what happens in the television industry. That is one program in one television medium. Think about all the actors who would have loved to audition for the role and were not given a chance to. Think about all the actors out there who didn't want to audition for the role (and there are a lot of them); if you analyze all those numbers, mathematically you start to realize your odds are not very good.

So, my feeling is you should accept this fact. You can certainly challenge it, but don't be affected by it; deal with it. Realize that these are the numbers you are working with. Let it motivate you. Let it change your philosophical approach to each individual audition. Take it for what it is worth. If you believe that the audition is merely an opportunity to display your potential as an actor, and if you are grateful for that opportunity, then your expectation will be met and your immediate goals fulfilled as you walk out of the casting director's office. You will not be leaving the office filled with anxious wondering: How did you do in the audition? Will you get any feedback? When will you hear about callbacks? You will not be concerned about those things.

I am not suggesting that this is an easy concept to grasp. How can you possibly accept the fact that you will not succeed? That you are not talented enough as an actor to get the job? I am not saying either of those things. I am merely being realistic. There are so many factors that are involved in a casting decision for a television program. In addition to the pure numbers game, a majority of those factors do not have anything to do with you. Let me repeat that: Many times, the reason you do not get a role, or even a callback for a role, has nothing to do with you personally.

I know that is an amazing concept to grasp—that there are decisions being made about you that have nothing to do with you—but it is true. The decisions are based on factors that include physical requirements like height, or the need for a resemblance to other actors on the show (e.g., a sibling or child). Sometimes it has to do with a change in the prototype of the character, so that by the time you audition, you are no longer suited to the role. Many times it has to do with a casting director's perception of your specific audition. I am a human being, not a computer. I get paid for my opinion, my perception. I am not always right. I can't be. I would like to think that I am more times than not, but when you are dealing with people, anything can happen.

Let's look at it this way. Out of the five hundred actors I audition for a role, about twenty-five of those actors receive a callback. If I look back on my career so far, I would be foolish to think that for every role the best twenty-five were always given a callback and the other four hundred seventy-five were completely not right for the role. That's impossible. I can honestly look back and say that I gave callbacks to people who should have been let go, and passed on people who probably deserved a callback. There is nothing you can do about this. I wish it weren't the case, but it happens. It isn't a crime—those actors were not robbed of an opportunity, and that's just the way it is. Those actors were still given the chance to be seen and evaluated, and if that is what you go in looking for, then there is a measure of success to that. Consider it one step in the right direction.

What I am suggesting is that any given audition is one step in a long line of steps needed for success. One must realize that a successful career as an actor is a long, ongoing process. Every audition, every acting class, every theatrical production is another moment in that process. From my perspective, the casting director–actor relationship is one that should be developed over a period of time. Every audition is a step toward defining that relationship. I will further explain this in chapter 33, "Building a Relationship with the Casting Director."

Free Yourself by Removing Expectations

If you can accept and apply this philosophy—that you are not going to get the job—you will actually be free to audition better. If you remove expectations, you will learn to enjoy the process and have fun. Actors who have fun in an audition are more likely to succeed and be remembered. As you continue to have more auditions, you will continue to develop without any greater expectations than to enjoy the experience, show potential, and develop the casting director–actor relationship.

Now, imagine if you actually show enough potential to receive a callback, or even book the job. Then, that result will be unexpected and that much more appreciated. Think about the entire enjoyment factor for a moment. Think of it from the casting director's point of view. Casting directors have to sit through many auditions—in this particular case, five hundred of them. Think about what that is like. The repetition of a scene being done that many times can drive some people crazy. As a casting director, I know the statistics show that the majority of actors auditioning for the role will not be physically right for that role. With that in mind, I would love for actors to come in and just enjoy themselves. If an actor enjoys himself, then I am going to enjoy myself and enjoy the experience. If I enjoy the audition, I am more likely to write something positive about that audition and the actor. I am not saying that person will book the job, or even get a callback. What I am suggesting is that the actor will be remembered, and that is what you ultimately want.

When I get a new role to work on, I review my notes on all the previous roles that are similar to the current role. If I see that an actor had a fun audition in the past, I am more likely to bring him in for the new role, even if he is not quite right for it. I will give him the benefit of the doubt on this new role. At the very least, he will have fun, and I will enjoy seeing him with the new audition material. If he comes in and shows he is right for the role, even better.

Offer Your Gift

One of my theatre mentors, Paul Austin, told me that auditioning is an opportunity for actors to present their gift. That gift is your craft, your talent. I say, keep offering your gift, and hopefully, one day someone will like what you are giving. In short, prepare the audition in the simplest, most specific manner possible. Create an environment that shows your potential. Use that audition experience to help better understand your application of craft, and the audition process. When you leave the audition, forget about the audition.

Begin to understand the business that trying to get an acting job on television is. Forget it in the sense that the audition is over and you can no longer do anything about it. But remember it as an educational tool. Make it an experience to learn from and build on. Analyze it. Ask yourself, "What mistakes did I make?" "Did I apply all of the choices from my rehearsal time that I wanted to make?"

After your self-analysis is over, forget that there was an actual role out there that was available to you. Don't fantasize about playing it or the accolades that might have come with it. When you are asked how the audition went, tell people it was fun.

Keep offering your gift. One day, you will walk into an audition, you will be prepared and gracious and good, and you will happen to be exactly the physical type that they are casting for, and you will get a callback. Maybe even book the job. If that happens, then someone has truly accepted the gift of your talent.

CHAPTER 4

Chances of Booking the Job

Let me continue with the numbers game and discuss some other factors that go into the casting decisions. Once again, I will talk in terms of a contract role on daytime television. It is important for you to understand what a casting director's process is for you to get a sense of how many people are actually involved in the ultimate decision of who receives a role.

A Casting Director's Process

My process begins when the executive producer tells me we are adding a new character to the show. Sometimes it isn't a new character, but a character who has been on the show before, who is now coming back played by a different actor. Sometimes a plot line in a daytime television show will require that a young character become older, and we need to cast a new, older actor to play that role. Regardless of the scenario, the process for me as a casting director is the same.

I receive a character description from the head writer, along with an audition scene to read with the actors. I release the character description to all the talent agents and managers in the industry through Breakdown Services. For those of you who do not know what that is, Breakdown Services is an independent company that e-mails agents and managers the character descriptions and specifics of the role that casting directors are currently looking for. The talent agents and managers will then mail to me their submissions of headshots and resumes of actors they would like me to consider for this role. The submissions usually trickle into my office over the next few days to a week. While that is happening, I am looking at my notebook for every role I have ever cast that was similar to this new role in type, age, and description. I create a list of those actors to now consider for this role. Many of these actors may not be available, but, to be thorough, I check with their representatives. This review of the old lists is the moment—which I talked about in the last chapter—when I will remember that a given actor had fun at a previous audition. I usually now put him on the new list.

Once the pictures have arrived at the office, the casting staff organizes them. I go through the pictures and pick people who I would like to have a pre-screen with. As mentioned in the previous chapter, a pre-screen is the first audition for any specific role. I will determine who will receive a callback from those pre-screens. The actors chosen are usually a combination of actors who I have read before and many actors who I will be meeting for the first time. In New York, I will read approximately two hundred actors for the role.

Out of the two hundred actors who get a pre-read, only about ten will get a callback. Only 5 percent of the actors who come in to audition get a callback. So, those ten actors now have to come back and audition in front of the executive producer. Out of those ten actors, the executive producer may only like five. That is 50 percent for me, and I like those odds. Those five actors will receive a screen test for the role. I'll come back to that in a little while. Please note: These numbers are always changing, but for the purposes of this book I have used averages.

Next, I fly to Los Angeles and go through the same process. There are more actors there and I only have one week to work, so I really need to be efficient. I read about three hundred actors. Out of the three hundred actors in Los Angeles that I read, about fifteen to twenty get a callback. Because I am in Los Angeles and I am alone, I videotape the callback auditions. When I get back to New York, I sit down with the executive producer and we watch the tape. The executive producer then decides, out of the fifteen to twenty actors, how many will receive a screen test. We usually test approximately seven out of those fifteen to twenty actors. So, if you put those numbers together, you will see how I arrived at those unfavorable figures. Two hundred auditions in New York and three hundred in Los Angeles equals five hundred pre-read auditions. Ten callbacks in New York and twenty in Los Angeles equals thirty total callbacks. Five are chosen for a screen test from New York and seven out of Los Angeles, which equals twelve actors who get a screen test. Twelve out of five hundred still have some hope of getting the role. Ironically, when we finally arrive at the screen test, all twelve actors will inevitably tell me that they don't have much of a chance to get the role because we are testing so many actors. I always find this to be funny, because in my mind these actors have the best opportunity to receive the role; they have beaten out 488 other actors who would change places with them in a heartbeat. I guess it is all relative to one's perception in the moment.

The Decision-Makers

Once the screen test is complete, a decision has to be made. That decision is made by the executives of all of the companies involved with the production. You, the actor, have no control over their decision-making process, except for the work that you did, which is now being presented to them by videotape. Several video copies of the test scene are made and distributed to the executives who make this ultimate decision. Guiding Light is produced by Procter & Gamble Productions. There is an Executive-in-Charge of Production and a Director of Creative Affairs—both have a strong say in who will receive the role. We are on the CBS network, and CBS has a Senior Vice President of Daytime Programming and a Vice President of Daytime Programs. They also have a strong say. Additionally, there is a Director of Daytime Casting in New York, who provides her input. The executive producer, who I mentioned earlier, certainly has a very strong say. The program has a head writer and she also has a say. I am asked my opinion, and although my input is taken into consideration, the power of the decision really lives with the top executives previously mentioned. Sometimes they do not agree on which actor they like. Sometimes they do. Sometimes they all like the same person, but many times they are divided. Under those circumstances, they sometimes ask if they can see more people, but many times they come to some compromise. Think about this. You cannot control these decisions. These are important people, with opinions that are respected. You can only hope that their opinion is in your favor.

The Human Element

I want to tell you a real story that will highlight the uncertainty that the human decision-making process adds into all of this. This is specifically about me. I was working on a contract role one time, auditioning actors in Los Angeles. I had to determine who, out of the three hundred actors I was reading, would receive a callback for that role. When I am in Los Angeles, I work a little differently than when I am home in New York. I usually read people and take a lot of notes before I just give someone a callback outright. The reasoning behind this is that I only have the one week that I am there to get the work done. I don't have the luxury of bringing people back a second or third time to read with me if I am unsure about them for the role, or if I'm unsure about bringing them to the executive producer. I have the fifteen to twenty taped callback slots available to me and must choose the right actors to fit into those slots.

So, when I start reading actors in the beginning of the week, I take specific notes to refer back to. From those notes, I usually create "yes," "no," and "maybe" piles of actors. The "yes" actors are people who I am absolutely positive are right for the role and deserve a callback. Most likely, I will award them with a callback shortly after we meet. The "no" pile is comprised of actors who I am completely sure are not right for that role, or who are not ready to take on the challenge of a contract role. The "maybe" pile is the point of my story, because a majority of the actors I like for the role will be placed in the "maybe" pile as the week progresses. This pile is mostly comprised of actors who I am just not sure of, or who, because it is so early in the week for me, I am holding off on calling back because I am waiting to see if anyone else who is coming in will be better than they are. They are talented, they are physically close to what I may be looking for, and they gave a solid audition. Because I am out of town and have only the fifteen to twenty slots to work with, I have to be sure not to fill those slots in the first two days that I am there. I have auditions set up for myself from Monday through Thursday. So, as I get to the middle of the week, I start filling in the callback slots based on my review of the actors in the "maybe" pile. Slowly, I make choices that will allow people from the list to prepare for the callback, while also leaving enough opportunity for the remaining actors who have to audition at the end of the week.

Let me get back to the point of the story. This one time, I only had fifteen callback slots available due to the amount of time I had the camera crew and audition space available to me. It was late on Thursday, about 5:30 P.M., and I had filled up thirteen of the fifteen callback slots. If I chose to, I could fill in the remaining two slots. I checked my "maybe" pile again and realized I had only three actors left in that pile. I had auditioned my last actor of the day and was done with all of my pre-read auditions. I was very confident in the thirteen actors I had coming in to tape the next day, so I reviewed the "maybe" list, thinking that I should fill the remaining callback slots with actors only if I felt passionate about them. I reviewed the notes on those actors and decided that one had clearly made a positive impression on me and was worthy of a callback.

I called his agent and set him up for the next day. I had one slot remaining, with two actors left to choose from. I re-reviewed my notes and went back and forth in my own mind as to which one of these actors deserved the callback. Now, I could have done two things here: I could have not given anyone the callback and just taped fourteen actors, or I could have given both actors a callback and risked running over the time I had allotted because I had to tape one additional actor. I kept debating with myself over the pros and cons of each actor, comparing them to each other in my mind, analyzing my perception of their strengths and weaknesses as actors. Realize that I have met them both once, for about ten minutes each. I came to a decision and chose the actor I will now call Bill R. (a made-up name). I decided to choose Bill R. because my notes showed that he had done a very solid job in his pre-read and that I had asked him to try it several times, a few different ways, and each time he took my notes and applied them. I liked the fact that he took direction well, and I also liked the physical qualities he brought to the role. He had a look that was different from the look of all the men already on the show, and one that was different from the majority of other men already scheduled to have a callback. So, I called his agent and set him up for the next day. I was told he would be there. His agent has no idea that I had been contemplating not giving his client a callback; for that matter, neither did the actor himself. At the tape session, I felt confident about all my choices, and all the actors did a credible job, including Bill R.

That night I flew back to New York, and on Monday morning I headed to work with the tape in my hand, ready to show the executive producer the actors I liked in Los Angeles. The executive producer and I viewed the tape together, and he commented on the actors he would like to screen test as the callback tape progressed. When we got to Bill R.'s audition, the producer seemed interested and asked me about him. I told him what

I thought of his potential, and my experience with him over the past few days. I stressed that he gave a solid audition and took direction well, and that I liked that his look was different from that of anyone else on the show. He agreed with me on that point and liked the feedback I gave him, so he decided to screen test Bill R. for the role. This is amazing if you think about it, because there I was, a few days earlier, contemplating whether I should give him a callback or pass on him; now here I was, knowing he would be getting an offer to screen test for the role. I was happy about this. This is the way the process works.

The screen test was scheduled for a few weeks later. Bill R. and the other twelve actors came to New York to test with an actress from the show. They all went through a long process that will be discussed later in the book. All of the executives then received a copy of the screen test day and had to make their decisions. They started asking about Bill R. and commented on the chemistry he had with his screen test partner. They liked him, as well as two other men, and after a few days of meetings and discussions, they decided to hire Bill R. They called to tell me the news that Bill R. was the actor they wanted the contract to go to, and told me that I should inform the agent and the actor.

Congratulations to Bill R.! Another actor has gone through the process and gotten himself a job. The amazing thing about this is, I almost didn't even give him a callback. He was thirty seconds away from being overlooked. I could have gone with the other actor on the "maybe" list, but I didn't. I could have passed on Bill R. completely. Does this make me a brilliant casting director because I gave him a callback? No. Would I have been a bad one if I didn't give him a callback? No, I don't think so, either.

The Role is Up for Grabs

If Bill R. wasn't in the screen test, I am sure someone else would have gotten the role. This is just the way it is and how it works. If this role was truly meant for Bill R., we would have had the original screen test without him and perhaps not made a decision on any of the actors in that first group. This would have initiated a second screen test. That second screen test would be comprised of new actors whom I would have auditioned, and certainly would have included the Los Angeles–based actors I placed on my "maybe" list—and most definitely Bill R., because he would have come so close the first time. That wasn't the case, though, and things worked out the way they did for him.

My point is simple. What if I hadn't given Bill R. a callback? Chances are he would have never been given the opportunity to receive that role. If he had been anxious about his audition, hanging on to the need for positive feedback and immediate results, and I had decided not to give him the callback, all the worrying in the world wouldn't have helped him to get a callback. He would have caused himself unnecessary stress, because he was obviously good enough to get the job. If he accepted my philosophy—that you can't control the decision-making process and should just be grateful for the opportunity—then he would have moved on from the audition, and if he didn't receive a callback, he wouldn't take it personally. If he didn't worry about receiving a callback, and he eventually did receive that call, then he would be in the same position he ended up in, minus the negative state of mind. Think about it: He went from being moments away from not receiving the callback to actually getting the job. My own decision-making process was the thing that determined his level of success, or lack thereof, for that specific opportunity.

Bill R. certainly had to be ready to succeed; after all, he was the one who actually had to perform, and he was rewarded with the role. This time the audition process had a positive result for Bill R., but for most actors, most of the time it does not. You can't control the decision-making process, but you can control the actual audition. The technique I will be discussing in the book will help you control what is controllable with the hope that you can better direct the human decision-making process to be in support of you.

CHAPTER 5

First Audition

There are two different kinds of first auditions that we need to discuss. Type A is the first time you ever audition for a casting director, when you have never met that casting director before, and B is the first time you are auditioning for a specific role, but when you have previously met the casting director. Let's discuss audition type A first, because without this, you may never get to audition type B.

Type A: The Audition and Meeting

The first time you meet a casting director is your first step toward building a working relationship with that person. If you believe in my philosophy, you will not be consumed with thoughts about the actual role that may be available to you. For the record, some casting directors will just have a meeting the first time they meet an actor if there is not a role available at that time, and sometimes it is a combination of both a meeting and a reading. The meeting part is important because this is where a casting director will get a sense of you as a person. In a sense, it is an opportunity for him to evaluate your personality. Because of that, you want to be on your best, most charming behavior. You do not have to worry about technique for the moment; just concentrate on being yourself. At the very basic level, television casting directors are looking for charming and personable people. Look at any successful sitcom—*Friends, Cheers, Seinfeld, Will & Grace*— the casts are incredibly charming and likeable; that is why we watch them. In daytime television, the most romantic leading men are the most charming characters; even the villains on the show are very personable. You love to hate them so much you have to watch them because of their charm and personality. Don't get me wrong; the casts for the above-mentioned shows are also extremely talented and funny. They are good at what they do, and that is the reason for their sustained success. However, in the early stages of many young actors' careers, many are given opportunities to audition based on their personality.

You cannot teach or fake charisma. However, everyone has a personality and the ability to be charming. What you must do is remind yourself not to allow your nerves or expectations to shut down your personality. Your personality is unique to you, and you must let that show while taking a meeting with a casting director and while auditioning. Many actors get trapped by the pressures of the audition and close off their personality. This does not serve you. Conversely, trying too hard to be personable will backfire on you every time. In my experience, actors who try to be overly friendly or funny never leave a positive impression—just a desperate one. Just be courteous, gracious—and yourself. That is the best advice. Your personality will give the casting director a clearer idea of the types of roles that you are right for. Chances are you will not be completely right for the first audition you have for a casting director. So, that casting director will take the opportunity to evaluate your reading and you for more suitable roles in the future. That is what the focus of audition type A is. The remainder of this chapter will apply to both audition types A and B.

Showing Potential is the Key

As mentioned in chapter 2, "An Audition is Not a Performance", your focus on the first audition should be on showing potential in the role. The technique will allow you to prepare yourself by setting obtainable audition goals for the first audition. You must trust that the casting director has an imagination and can visualize you in the role. It is your responsibility to help the casting director visualize that by showing the potential you could have in the role. That potential will breed confidence in you. I am a strong believer that a good audition technique will give you confidence. If you have confidence in yourself, chances are a casting director will have that same confidence in you.

You want to be presented in a way that the casting director can see you growing in the role. Don't give a performance that is striving for all the levels that the character could be. Be honest to the text in your hands. Striving for anything more is too much. You cannot display what the character will become because, in truth, the development of the character happens when the actual actor is cast. His persona and interpretation, in combination with the writers' and producers' vision, will determine what the character will become. Concentrate on the sides given to you.

As a casting director, I am looking for two things. One, is the actor physically what I am looking for? Right age, hair color, height, eye color, et cetera? And two, is he a good actor? Does he have skills? Is he multi-faceted with the audition material? Does he look like what I like to call a "thinking, feeling, and living being"? These are characters that have sincere and simple thoughts, accompanied by legitimate feelings. Those feelings need to be appropriate to the tone of the audition material. This creates levels in the reading.

Pay specific attention to what I am about to write, as it is a valuable distinction you should understand before we get into the main technique part of this book. Casting directors are not specifically looking for technique, but rather the results of the technique itself. I am never observing an actor and trying to analyze what specific technique he is using. The truth is, there are so many techniques and variations of the same technique that I would go crazy trying to determine that. The same holds true for what kind of acting training one might have. It is something that is not that important to me in the actual moments of observation. The *results* are important. That the actor has a technique is the factor that allowed him to be in a position to succeed in the audition. What I mean by "succeed" is that he was a thinking, feeling, and living being with purpose as a character. The technique is what you use in your preparation, and it is what you rely on in the moment of the actual in-the-room auditions.

You want to make a memorable impression by doing solid, simple, and specific work. Not *unusual*, but *interesting* work. You accomplish this by being well prepared, knowing where your acting moments are, and still being available to let things happen in the room. Many actors tell me they just wing it in an audition. Some people are very good at that; others are terrible. In my opinion, the actor who is better prepared for the audition is in a better position for spontaneous interaction in the actual reading. The thinking for me in an audition is that the actor should try to *make* it happen, not try to *let* it happen. You must be focused and natural and committed to your choices, but also available to make adjustments in the moment. This is completely different advice than what I would say to actors in a theatrical production.

Theatrical Preparation versus Audition Preparation

The rehearsal of a play is where the choices are made, worked on, developed, and changed. The performances are where the cast can let it happen, to let themselves be available to the unknown, relying on the structure of the show's blocking, its technical aspects, and the acting collaboration they worked through in rehearsals. They are prepared for it, but are still looking for something new to happen every night.

In the audition, you must know what you want to happen and try to make those moments happen, while still being available to the unexpected moments. In a theatrical preparation, one might use sense memory work and use something from one's own history to help better understand how the character behaves in the circumstances provided. This is a great technique that I believe in—just not for the television audition.

The need for that theatrical preparation is unfounded because of the true lack of time one might have to prepare for the television audition. To truly be prepared for a theatrical event, an actor would rehearse for several weeks, going through lots of ups and downs in terms of commitment to the choices and the embodiment of those choices before feeling ready to perform those choices. In a television audition, the actor must make quick choices and stick to those choices with the ambition of getting through the first round of audition screening. You have three minutes to show yourself and your work. That's a real challenge, and you may never do that material again. So, you make appropriate choices that serve you for that specific opportunity. Have a plan and stick to it.

As mentioned earlier, you cannot rely on the other person. There is no opportunity to collaborate on your choices with the other person (reader). If you are collaborating with an actor friend who is helping you prepare for the audition, you are setting yourself up for failure, because you can not be sure the reader is making the same choices as your friend, if any. Auditioning is about *you*. All your choices should be made accordingly.

An Audition is Not Workshop Time

A reminder: The first audition is not a workshop time for you and the casting director. Do not think of the casting director as a director (even though many are) or an acting coach. It is true that casting directors will give notes and direction, but we are not looking to collaborate like a theatre director would. We do not have time, and more, importantly, it is not the true function of the job, especially at the first audition. As you move to the callback stage and beyond, a casting director will take on more of that role. Truthfully, a casting director will only give direction and begin to collaborate if he sees potential for you in the role. It comes back full circle to *potential*. Potential resonates from an actor who makes choices for himself and has a plan for the character in the audition. For your part, you must recognize that your objective is to be seen and be remembered. Part of having a plan is to know what you want to say and do when you get in the room. You will be remembered more for your acting choices than for your conversation, questions, and verbal insights concerning the character and story.

Memorization

A quick thought on memorization. I mentioned in an earlier chapter that I prefer for actors to hold their sides during the audition. I feel that actors in their first audition should be very familiar with the dialogue of the audition scene. In a sense, they can have a large portion of the material memorized, but I still prefer and recommend that you hold the sides. It reminds us that it is an audition and not a performance; it allows you to refer back to the page for those moments that you might be unclear on, or perhaps when nerves get in the way. When I break down the technique, you will see how valuable a tool your sides will become.

Type B

The type B audition is really an opportunity for the casting director to keep an eye on your development as an actor. If you are given the opportunity to audition for a casting director several times, it just means that he likes what he sees and is trying to find the most appropriate role for you to hopefully book. This is a good thing; do not get frustrated by the number of times you have to keep coming back for the same casting director, because it marks progress in your own development and in the casting director–actor relationship. It takes some actors years of auditioning for the same casting director before landing a job through him. This is simply a function of looking for the right role at the right time, and you being ready for it.

CHAPTER 6

The Callback

The callback is an excellent indication that you are doing something positive, both in the advancement of your skill level and in the advancement of your technique. As in the case of the first audition, there are two kinds of callbacks. They are both favorable. For our purposes, I will label them "callback type 1" and "callback type 2." Let's discuss type 1 first.

Type 1

Type 1 is a callback for the casting director. In my experience, this happens quite a bit. What this usually means is that your first audition went well, but there may be something that is getting in the way of the casting director awarding you a callback for the producer (callback type 2). I can speak from my own experience and tell you that this usually has more to do with the casting director than with the actor. A second reading for me is the thing that usually allows me to have confidence in my opinions, whether that opinion is in your favor or not. When this type of callback is about the actor, it is usually just an opportunity to give the actors on the previously mentioned "maybe" list the benefit of the doubt, to see if they can come in an exceed the previous expectations and results of the first audition.

Another reason why I might choose to bring someone back in for myself would be if someone meets the physical requirements of the role I am searching for, but her first audition was not up to par. I still might give the actress a second chance with a callback because of her look. The thinking is that perhaps that person was just having an off day when I met her the first time.

Many times, a casting director will callback an actor because he wants to give some specific direction and see if the actor can apply that direction to the audition material. Any of these examples are possible. They all mean the same thing: that you showed potential in your first audition and are worthy of another opportunity to advance. You are making progress and moving one step closer to the ultimate goal of booking a job.

Type 2

Type 2 is when you are asked to come back for the executive producer. In my primetime experience, the writer and the director have been present with the producer in a type 2 callback. In daytime television, it is always and only the executive producer. Because I am currently in daytime television, I will just be writing with the executive producer in mind. When you receive a direct-to-producer callback, it simply means that the casting director has confidence in what you did in your first audition—that you met any physical requirements associated with the role, and you displayed sound technique as an actor and an auditioner. The casting director can visualize you in the role and as part of the cast.

Don't Change Your Choices

How do you proceed from the first audition to the callback, hoping that you will be considered for a screen test? In my opinion, the key to the callback is to keep making progress from the first audition. You are being asked back because you did something good. In your first audition, you showed promise as yourself playing this character. So you have to make sure that you keep that potential. As a casting director, I want to see pretty much what I have previously seen. I don't expect the actor to make drastic changes to the audition because he is going to the producer now. I do hope that the actor continues to work on the sides, but that he does not change his major choices unless directed to do so. I only want him to sharpen his first audition.

Let me put it another way. If I were interested in buying a car and went to a dealership to test-drive several cars, at some point I would make up my mind about which car was my favorite, and perhaps decide to buy. Lets say there is one car I really like; it's red and has power windows, an automatic transmission, and a lot of state-of-the-art items. Perhaps I decide to come back the next day with my wife. All night I have told her about this great red car, telling her how I feel about it and how great it would be to own it. However, when we get to the dealership, the salesman tells me that the red car is gone, but he has the exact same one in blue. That is not the car I was interested in buying, and not the car I was trying to sell my wife on.

In casting and callbacks it is the same thing. If I liked what you were selling in your first audition in my office, I expect that the same audition will drive into the producer's office. Chances are, I have been talking you up to the executive producer, raving about you as an actor, about your experience and training, and about how your first audition went. Perhaps I even gave him my reasons why I decided to give you a callback. If you drive in with a different audition, the producer will question me on what I observed in your first audition. In a sense, I am selling to him what you were selling to me. If I am expecting the red car, I want to see the red car. Don't think you have to turn a red car blue. Instead, think about polishing the red car up so it shines. Okay, I am done with this metaphor—but I must warn you that I will have more in the book, since I like to use them.

How to Make Progress from Potential

I have a very simple rule for how the actor should prepare for his or her progression from first audition to the callback. If you received notes on your first audition, then work hard at applying those notes. If you did not receive a note on something that you did, then leave it alone. Assume that it is exactly the way the casting director would like you to present it to the executive producer. The mistake that I find a lot is that many actors do not progress from their callback to the next level because they do not maintain the potential of the first audition. It is my advice that the actor should just keep the original choices fresh by having confidence in those choices and by becoming more familiar with those choices through repetition and rehearsal. In an effort to stay prepared, an actor can make the mistake of rein-terpreting the character by changing the original choices. This also happens because the actor focuses so much on the notes that the casting director gave him to work on that the moments that were not given any notes seem to get forgotten. The actor then loses the potential that he previously displayed. The actor must realize that he is one step closer in the process, and that a radical change is not required here.

If your first audition was 75 percent successful, then you only received notes on the remaining 25 percent of the material. That would be a productive first audition. If you then work so hard on the 25 percent of the audition that you received direction on that you forget to keep the remaining 75 percent at the level of freshness it had, then you will only have a 25 percent successful callback. What good is that? That is how most actors do not get to the next level. They forget to keep what they had from first audition in the callback. In the casting director's view, they haven't grown, even though they may have taken and applied the notes as asked of them. That the actor was unable to display the potential previously shown will outweigh the positive fact that he took direction and applied it. Of course, many actors do not progress from the first audition to the callback because they cannot apply the notes that were given to them at all. They may keep the potential that they had in the first audition, but fail to apply the direction. This too is viewed as a lack of development.

Many times I will like someone at a first audition and then work with him at that audition on the moments that I think he needs some help on. If I feel satisfied that he was able to accomplish what I was looking for, or at least get close to it, I will award him a callback. The assumption is that he will get better as he continues to prepare for the callback, and I will encourage him to do so. However, at the callback, he may either revert back to the level of his first audition—which is not good enough now—or he may lose the potential that was previously there because of the extra focus on the notes.

Actors who can sustain their potential or even improve from their first audition to the callback will be considered for the next level. Realize that, in the real world, the producers are not analyzing this development from one stage to another stage; they are just studying the audition that is in front of them. I am breaking down the analysis of each stage of progression for you in the book so you can look at it from a more detail-oriented perspective.

Your Callback Audition for a New Role

Here is a bit more philosophy. Earlier, I mentioned that the key to a successful career and auditioning is the recognition that it is a long, ongoing process. You need to remember this as a motto for enduring success. Most actors do not receive a callback for the first role they audition for with a specific casting director, but instead receive one in the form of a new opportunity for a completely different role. When the casting director has a new role two weeks, two months, two years down the road, and you are right for that role, you will be considered for it largely on the basis of the first audition for the previous role. Are you following me? In essence, you will receive your callback for your first role by getting an opportunity to audition for a new role.

The Perception of You Changes

When you receive a callback, you have gained a level of success separating you from all the actors who auditioned for that role. The group that gets called back is made up of a very small percentile. I would say you are now in the top 5 percent. This does not guarantee success, but it does make the impression of you change. Also, in my opinion, once you have received a callback from a casting director, the casting director will look at you in a different way. I definitely do this. When an actor has made it to the callback round for me on a role but does not get the role, I often will immediately reward him with a callback for a new role, without the need for another first audition. In many cases, the actor has earned that right. I hold him in higher esteem. When his agent submits him for a new role and I see his headshot and resume, I register in my mind that he has gone further in the process with me than many other actors, and I usually put that picture in a separate pile. If you make it to that separate pile, you have acquired a level of success with me. This is also considered progress in the ongoing development of the casting director–actor relationship.

Callback Memorization

In regards to memorization, I feel that at the callback stage you should be 90 percent off book, but still using the sides during the audition. In the best-case scenario, I envision an actor who is memorized, but is also turning the pages during the audition, almost turning the pages without looking directly at them. (The focus is on the reader.) If the actor then loses his place or his focus, I would like to think that he would be able to look down at his sides and be in the vicinity of the line he is searching for.

So, for the callback you should be extremely familiar with the lines, but still have the sides available in your hand if they are needed.

CHAPTER 7

The Screen Test

The hope of being in any callback situation is that you will make it to the next level and be chosen for a screen test for that role. As you get closer to the ultimate achievement of booking the job, there is more pressure on you to succeed and display yourself as an actor.

If you are fortunate enough to be chosen for a screen test, you must work even harder to present yourself as a more complete actor. If the first audition is about showing your potential for the role, and the callback is about keeping that potential while applying direction, then the screen test is the actual presentation of yourself as the role. It is the most performance oriented you must be to get the job, before actually doing the job. It is time to make the progression from audition to performance. This is when your knowledge of craft will be relied on and tested. It is true that you may get to this stage with just a good audition technique, but you will be very lucky to get the role without a true understanding of craft. The screen test will usually weed out those people if the earlier stages have not.

The Business Side

There are some business specifics that must be worked out before the test. Once I have contacted the actors we have decided to screen test for the role, our business affairs department negotiates a contract with their agents. Their salary over the course of their contract is determined before the test. At *Guiding Light*, we have a three-year contract commitment. This basically means that the actor is committed to the program for three years and is not allowed to do any other projects without the consent of the program. Once all the deals are closed, a screen test day is determined.

The Screen Test Day

At this point in the process, my work as a casting director is pretty much done. The actual actress or actor from the show who plays the other character in the audition scene will now read with the actors at the screen test. A director is hired for the day, and all the departments (hair, makeup, wardrobe) are involved. It is basically a very intense day of work for the actors. The twelve actors will arrive early in the morning for what is called "dry rehearsal." This is where the actors will read the scene for the first time with the real actress. The director will also give the actors their physical blocking at this time. While one actor is in dry rehearsal, another is in makeup, another in hair, and others in wardrobe. All twelve will rotate through all of these stations during the morning.

After everyone has completed the morning rehearsal, they arrive at the actual set. There, they review their blocking for the camera operators (camera blocking) and get familiar with the real set furniture and props, if there are any. After camera blocking, the first actor will do a dress rehearsal with the executive producer observing. Notes are given to the actor after the dress rehearsal and before the actual screen test taping. These notes will come from the producer and the director. The screen test is done one time, in one take. All twelve actors go right after each other. It is a long day for all the actors involved. The actors testing have performed the scene four times each. The actress from the show will perform that scene forty-eight times that day—think about how she feels! That is the process.

From Auditioning to Performing

For our purposes, you now have to move your focus from auditioning to performing. You have finally arrived at the moment to collaborate. You can see that there is not an extraordinary amount of time to do this. However, if you are prepared for the test, then you have made very clear and strong choices for what you would like to play. The director will be giving you assistance by giving you the physical movement necessary for the scene. The directorial guidance will feed off the strength of your choices. In your preparation for the screen test, you should now be incorporating all of the acting techniques you have acquired in your training as an actor. You want to prepare for this day like it is a one-act play that you have only one performance of. So, you must make sure that you have the emotional tools available to you that you would have when preparing for an actual theatrical performance. It is here that the actor should include acting methods and techniques to get ready for the actual scene. Also, the actor who is screen testing should realize that the actress who is in the scene with him is there to help him, and he should be available to any suggestions or instincts that the actress may have. This will go a long way toward displaying any kind of chemistry that the actor may have with that actress. Many times, the actress doing the screen test with the auditioners will be playing a major storyline with whoever receives the role. However, it is important to remember that this is still your job interview, and that you need to come in with strong, playable choices to display who you are as an actor.

Screen Test Memorization

I hope this does not need to be written, but you should be completely memorized for the screen test. This should be letter-perfect. You should not change any dialogue or improvise in the scene. Remember that the writers will see the test. I don't think you want to give them the impression that you are an actor who freely changes the lines of a scene to suit your own needs. Also, you must be able to project to the decision-makers that you are someone who handles memorization easily, because in daytime television there will be a lot of dialogue to remember every day.

CHAPTER 8

On the Clock

Now I want to start getting you ready for your first audition for a role by getting you disciplined in your preparation time and your technique. I like to use the term "On the Clock" in reference to the amount of time you have to apply your audition technique while preparing for the audition. If you are informed that you have an audition at my office at 12:00 P.M. tomorrow and it is 12:00 P.M. today, you are On the Clock for twenty-four hours. If you received the same call at 6:00 P.M., you would be On the Clock for twelve hours. What this means is that you are spending the majority of that time available to you preparing for the audition. Nothing should be considered more important to you than this audition opportunity. Now I know that life gets in the way some times, that many things can come up and be more pressing, but if you can accept the attitude that the clock is running and that you need to give it your focus, you will start becoming a more disciplined actor in terms of your preparation time and the application of a useable technique.

There are many points to the audition technique that I am going to be detailing in this book. Eventually, individual preference and application will determine how many of those points work best for you. Some actors may decide that all the points are easy to apply, while others may decide that only a handful are helpful. My hope is that all of the items will be of equal value and accessibility to you. Once you are familiar with the technique, you must then adapt it to the On the Clock time that is available to you for that specific audition. In a sense, you will have many versions to the technique: the twenty-four hour preparation version, the twelve-hour version, the two-hour version, and so on. This rule will also apply to cold readings, which I will further discuss in chapter 29. Your application of the technique will be determined by the amount of time left On the Clock.

Even if my specific technique in this book does not work for you, you must find one that does, and still keep the On the Clock discipline in mind for your career. The actor who is best prepared for the audition is the actor who is best prepared to succeed in the audition. If you can have success in the audition, you will be on your way to a successful career.

CHAPTER 9

General Audition Information and Advice

Before I get into the technique, I want to give some general advice that can be used for any type of television audition. This chapter will discuss the need for the actor to make specific and simple choices in regard to the backstory for his audition scene. I will also show you how to ask intelligent questions during your meeting and explain my feelings concerning how much physicality an actor should bring to an audition.

Make Specific Choices and Fill in All the Blanks

This section could also be called "Asking Yourself the Right Questions and Finding the Answers". The first thing you should do after reading the audition sides is to answer any questions that are not answered through the dialogue of the scene. Most audition scenes don't give much more information than a setting. I honestly feel like the actor should just create the backstory of the characters in the scene. There is no right answer here. Ask yourself, Who are these people? Ask yourself what has happened to these people before the scene begins. Stick to the answer you decide. The answers that you give yourself should be simple, direct, and useful.

Most actors create too much backstory. The audition is about the now—not the before and not the after; it's about the now! Most actors audition with so much baggage of a backstory that they never try to achieve anything in the course of the audition. They end up playing the residual subtextual feeling of the complicated choices they made, rather than actively pursuing the present objective. The truth is, as a casting director, I would much rather have an actor make choices, whether they are appropriate or not. Remember, you are not going to book this job anyway, so your concern that your backstory is not the backstory that the writer intended is a waste of your energy. If your backstory is appropriate to your choices and it assists you in your audition, it will create a solid audition, which is what we are looking for.

An Example of Who the Characters Are

Let me give you a hypothetical situation. Let's say you have sides that have a man and woman in the scene. It is clear that these two people have had a relationship, but the relationship is not clear to the actor from the dialogue and the action of the scene. There is no romance, or intimacy, or any mention of a relation to each other or to someone else. As an actor, make a choice. For example, decide for yourself whether these two people are brother and sister or husband and wife. To me it doesn't matter. If your choices are appropriate to the action in the scene, then it will be okay. If you can make the dialogue work in conjunction with your choices, then it works. The truth is if the backstory is so vital to the audition, you will be given the information when you get your sides. Or let's say that you are so right for this role—you are physically what we are looking for, the right height, age, et cetera. You made the choice that the audition scene involves a brother and a sister. It turns out that it is not a brother and sister scene, but a scene between a married couple. Believe me, I will find out what choices you made and make the adjustment to the backstory, so that we can do it again with the appropriate information.

However, I will only do that if you are what we are looking for and you showed potential in your audition to do the role—and, of course, you are a good actor. If you are the right type physically and do not show potential as an actor capable of playing that role, then I will probably dismiss you. If you are not the right type and don't show potential, then you certainly will be dismissed. Now, you are probably asking yourself, how can you not tell the difference between a brother and a sister scene and a husband and wife scene? One, you would be surprised at what might be assumed and not communicated to you, and two, I probably agree with you, but I am trying to make a point. That point is, if you trust the facts that are present in the dialogue of the sides, it is almost impossible to make a wrong choice as to who these people are.

An Example of What Happened

Once you decide who these people are, you must make choices about the backstory in terms of what has happened to the relationship. If you decide that the two people in the scene used to be in a romantic relationship, and it is clear from the dialogue that they are no longer in one, then you should decide what happened to them. However, your answer should be short and to the point. Many times, when I am teaching, actors will provide me with a very long-winded analysis of the steps leading up to the characters' breakup. The following is an example of things I have been told: "I decided that they were in a relationship, and she found out he was having an affair with her best friend after confronting him—he denied it at first, but then later admitted it. After he admitted it, she decided to move to New York City for a few months, but she is back now because she's pregnant with his child. . . ."

That is a lot of information for a three-page audition. It is way too much information. Truthfully, I wouldn't know or care if you determined that the man cheated on the woman with her best friend or her sister, or perhaps something different, like they broke up because the woman found out he was already a married man. Any of the choices are fine, because it only suits your needs for backstory and subtext. It doesn't suit my needs at all, except to know that you made a choice. If the actress had simply decided that they were in a relationship and it ended because he was cheating on her, that is enough. I don't need to know, and you shouldn't be concerned with too many specifics of that situation. What a casting director is looking for is the result of your choices. If the choices are tangible, then the action of the audition is clearer. If the choices are complicated, then having too much information slows the action of the scene down.

Once again, you will usually be provided with any pertinent information about the backstory and the relationship. If you decide that they broke up due to an affair and it turns out that the circumstances were different, you will get the correct information when the casting director deems that it is appropriate for you. You may never know the true backstory if you are not right for the role and never get a callback. This does not hinder your ability to make choices and show potential.

The point is to fill in the blanks. Make the choices you need to do an audition, and do it well. If the backstory is not given, make a simple and specific decision about who the characters are and what has previously happened to him that now allows the present scene to take place. What I like about this attitude is that it puts you in control of your audition and shows confidence. This leads me to the next section, "Asking Questions".

Asking Questions

Before I start this section, I want to be clear: Every actor who has an audition should and must feel confident that he has enough answers to any lingering questions he may have about the sides and the character. I like to make the actors feel comfortable before their audition and will usually ask a few conversational questions to relax the actor and to get to know him. However, as a casting director in the middle of hundreds of auditions, I prefer that actors not have any questions to ask about the reading before the reading. I would rather we just get to it. I like to see what an actor has prepared. It is my opinion that this safeguards the actor as well.

Let me try to clarify my somewhat contrasting statements. When the audition is about to start, I ask two questions of everyone: (1) Do you want to sit or stand? (2) Do you have any questions? I will always answer any questions that an actor has, but I really prefer an actor to just make choices and go for it. I am being honest. A lot of times, those choices are what makes the difference between you and the actor behind you. There is a certain level of confidence that an actor displays by saying, "I have made some choices." That is really what I am interested in.

I also am very hesitant to answer too many questions right before an audition. Most actors who ask questions either ask several questions or ask very long questions that require long answers. I get hesitant to answer such questions because in my mind, I am asking myself how this actor could possibly incorporate my answers in the ten seconds he has between my answer and the start of the audition. If you appreciate the craft of acting and the process one must go through to prepare for an audition, you should recognize that those answers cannot be used effectively. It puts the casting director in a position of turning the audition into a work/rehearsal session, and that is the furthest thing from what an audition is.

By no means would I have the time to allow the actor to re-prepare for the audition by incorporating my answers. I want to be honest here. Sometimes I even get a little irritated that I am doing the actor's homework. I don't want to perceive that an actor has not prepared for the audition, but that is how I feel sometimes when an actor asks so many questions. There is a big difference between my perception of an actor who says, "I don't have any questions. I made some choices," and my perception of the actor who says, "Tell me about this character," "Who are these people?" or "What happened to the characters before this scene starts?" You want to safeguard yourself against any negative perceptions about you. Don't let the casting director think that you did not do your homework, whether you did or not.

If I tell you that the character is a thirty-two-year-old divorced mother of two with a drinking problem, and you thought she was a happily married woman who runs a daycare center, then you are going to be totally thrown from what you prepared. I would rather see what you prepared! The point is, if you can't figure out who the person is from the given dialogue, then you are misdirected anyway. Also, remember that you are not going to book the job, so you might as well play your choices. You can always come back another day with the appropriate backstory and character if you are asked to, if you are physically right and showed potential as an actor.

A Solution to the Challenge

Now, for those of you who feel that I am being harsh here, let me give you a solution that I absolutely love. If you *have* to, or *want* to, or *need* to ask a question, then ask a multiple-choice question, or what I call an "A/B question." If an actor asks a question and gives me the option of two possible answers, then I feel more comfortable in giving an answer. It also clearly says to me, "This actor has worked on the audition, and this is the last bit of information she is looking for to have a successful audition." Basically, when an actor asks an A/B question, she is telling me that she has two auditions prepared: the A version and the B version. For example, "Rob, I have only one question. Are the characters (A) brother and sister or (B) husband and wife?" This tells me that if I give answer (A), the actor will go down *that* path for the audition. If I give answer (B), then she will give *that* version.

The multiple-choice question accomplishes many things. (1) It satisfies an actor's need to ask the question. (2) It displays the knowledge that the actor has prepared for the audition. (3) It shows that the actor has made other choices about the character and story and is confident in those choices. (4) It puts the casting director in a comfortable position while answering a question right before the audition begins.

So, if you have to ask a question, ask a multiple-choice question. But just ask one.

Sit or Stand; It's Your Choice

This is easy. I feel that the best auditions are when the actor sits or stands. It doesn't matter which one. My preference is that the actor chooses whatever makes her feel the most comfortable. Actors constantly ask me what my preference is. My preference is that you feel comfortable in the audition, and unless I have some specific reason why I would want you to sit or stand, you should just do the one you want. I certainly will ask an actor to do it the opposite way if I like her first audition and think she could benefit from the adjustment.

My biggest suggestion is that you do it the way you've practiced it. If you practiced standing in your studio apartment, don't sit in the casting director's office. If you practiced sitting, don't feel the need to stand during the audition. Your body will naturally start adjusting and find comfort through repetition. If you decide to break the repetition and do something other than what your body has practiced, your instrument will begin to compensate during the audition. If you stick to what you have prepared, it will bring familiarity to the audition when nerves could create problems.

Along these same lines, try not to practice in unorthodox ways. Don't run lines while eating dinner, lying on your sofa, or standing on your head—unless you think you will do that in casting director's office . . . which you shouldn't be doing.

Some actors feel that sitting or standing is a key to the audition. At least, their behavior makes me think that, since they spend so long deciding what they should do. It's not. As with the backstory, make a choice stick to it. This also gives you confidence and control. Confidence and control are two things that I am very much in favor of actors having, and two things I urge you to think about. I am not suggesting that you should be stiff in the chair, or that when standing, you restrict your natural gestures. You should be active in the space you are occupying. Your behavior should be appropriate to the feelings of the scene, and you should let your body react accordingly. So, if you want to sit and you don't see a chair, ask for one. If you take a seat at the start of the meeting and you would rather stand before you start reading, then do so.

Many actors get hung up on whether or not there is a preference. As hard as auditioning is, why do most actors focus on the small stuff? Let me just say one thing. I have never hired or not hired an actor because she stood during the audition or sat during the audition. I have never given a callback or not given a callback to an actor because she stood during the audition or sat during the audition. I have never denied an actor advancement in the process because she stood and I thought she should have sat. What is most important to me is that her focus is toward the reader and she feels comfortable.

Empower yourself.

No Blocking

An actor has great control over the focus that the audition should have. Because I feel that focus is so vital to the audition, I also say, "No blocking, no props, no miming."

When you are auditioning, the casting director is looking at you. Your face, your body, your thoughts and feelings are all being observed. When you stand or sit in place, you are forcing the focus to be directly on those attributes. You are not distracting yourself from your own choices. When you block out your movement in an audition, it can do several negative things. First and most obviously, it draws focus away from you. When I see someone make deliberate movement, I begin to watch the movement. It is natural for me to do that. Is that what you want me watching in your audition? I hope not. It also suggests that you have spent too much time working on the areas of the audition that you should not be focusing on when you are at home and On the Clock. If you spent an hour blocking your audition scene, that is a wasted hour that could have been spent on incorporating your acting choices so that you feel comfortable with them. I wonder sometimes whether an actor subconsciously feels that if she shows a casting director she can block a scene, the casting director will be confident that she will be able to do her own blocking on the set. If that is the case, it is really putting the cart before the horse. Remember, this is not a theatrical production. It does not need all the aspects of a finished product.

Let's think about the physical space for a moment. There is limited available space in most casting directors' offices (mine included). If you block out your audition scene with a lot of movement and then you arrive in my office—which probably does not have the space that you have become accustomed to—your concentration will be thrown off. Why would you want to take a chance on that happening? You should prepare your audition with the least amount of obstacles. If this scenario took place, I would only see an actor who was either nervous or perhaps lacked focus. Meanwhile, unbeknownst to me, the actor is thrown off because she cannot complete the blocking that was prepared.

You want your *acting* to be evaluated, not your staging ability.

A Blocking Mistake

Let me tell a quick story highlighting what not to do. If you watch daytime television, many times an actor will be talking to another actor with her back to that person. The actor will walk downstage toward a camera, almost looking at the camera, while the other person in the scene remains in the background, looking and listening in the direction of the actor. This bit of blocking is done specifically for the camera, with the director's hope of achieving a close-up on one actor while still viewing the other person's reaction within one television frame.

Once, in my office, an actor actually did that blocking. He was sitting in front of me, with his focus toward me (I was the reader), and when we got to a very serious beat in the script, he got up out of the chair and walked toward a wall at the side of my office, with his back toward me. He proceeded to complete the audition in this manner, with the occasional glance back over his shoulder toward me. I realized after the audition that he was trying to present himself as he would be on the set. Consciously or not, he was trying to express to me that he was a professional who knew what he was doing in the medium. Meanwhile, I was sitting at my desk reading lines to someone whose back was toward me. How absurd. Needless to say, he did not get a callback for the role.

I stated earlier that the way you audition for a role and the way you perform a role are different. This is proof of that. Why would this actor sacrifice the focus I had on him to do that form of blocking? This was completely unnecessary, and it actually sabotaged his reading.

No Props

The same theory of distraction applies to the actor who introduces props into the audition. Let me remind you that we are talking about a television audition. Perhaps this rule does not apply to theatre auditions. Anyway, when an actor introduces a prop, my focus goes to that prop. Why do you want to draw focus away from yourself? Your cell phone is not looking for a job—you are. But if you pull out your cell phone, I will look at your cell phone. Ten seconds looking at your cell phone is ten seconds the casting director is not looking at you. In a two-minute audition, ten seconds is a lifetime. Also, in regard to craft, I would think that one would have to practice for many, many hours to naturally incorporate a prop into an audition. Just as if you were performing a play, it might take weeks of the rehearsal period to feel comfortable with certain props. Why introduce an element that is not 100 percent fail-safe and 100 percent necessary for success? I hate audition scenes where the character is on a phone. I also understand that there is an exception to every rule—the use of a cell phone might be one of them—but I really do have an imagination and can see past whether there is an actual phone present or not. If you feel it is a necessary to introduce a prop like that, then use it sparingly. Don't make your reading all about the prop.

A Prop Mistake

It's time for another quick story. Once, in the middle of an audition, an actor pulled out his wallet and started counting his money. This was not written in the scene, but rather the actor's choice, which makes it even worse. He was having a fairly positive audition up to this point. He wasn't physically exactly what I was looking for, but he was in the ballpark. So, he casually and naturally pulled out his wallet and started counting his money. I must admit that he did introduce it nicely into his audition. However, when his audition was done (and he did use the wallet until the sides were completed), I knew he had forty-three dollars in his wallet.

Think about it. No matter how much money an actor has in his wallet, is that what you want me to know about your work? He spent so much time with the prop that I couldn't help looking at the prop, and counting his money with him. I was distracted, because he distracted me. He actually distracted himself from his acting choices for the audition. He might as well have announced that he was pulling out his wallet to count his money. I wasn't that interested in him to begin with, because he was only physically close to what I was looking for, and after the audition, I didn't know what his character wanted from the scene. The audition was a wasted opportunity because of the use of a prop. Now, if the prop had never come out, we might have done the scene again, or perhaps he might even have been given a callback. I don't know. What I do know is that my focus would still have been on him, and not his wallet. With a waiting room full of people, I wasn't interested enough to start over with him not doing that. I needed to move on.

No Miming

Along the same lines, don't behave like a mime in an audition. It is distracting. Every young actor, at one point or another, has taken out an imaginary pitcher of water and "poured" it into an imaginary glass for some acting class exercise. Some have even ventured to drink the imaginary water, too. This has led some actors to incorporate fake props or actions in their auditions. Practicing these kinds of exercises for an audition is a waste of time. Once again, I have never hired or given a callback to anyone who has done such theatrical tricks. Now, if you are what we are looking for, then perhaps we'll do it again without that distraction, but I think you get my point.

Keep the focus on you and your choices. Auditioning is hard enough; don't make it harder on yourself. If you need these tricks to feel like you'll have a successful audition, then I suggest you need to question yourself and the choices you make in your preparation for the audition.

CHAPTER 10

The Audition Technique

Okay, let's get technical. This chapter and the next several comprise the heart and the purpose of the book. I wanted to write this book to give actors a specific audition technique that I feel would put them in the best position to succeed in each individual audition as well as in their careers. Remember that this is the technical side to the audition. This is the part that is done at home, when working and preparing for your audition. The more you apply the technique and practice with the technique, the quicker it will become second nature to you in the actual room while actively auditioning.

Of course, your acting training will complement the technique. However, this book does not teach the acting part, which is what you must bring to the work. The acting part fills in the blanks around the technique. This book does not teach acting; the assumption is that your craft is in place and ready to combine with an audition technique.

I first realized that a lot of actors audition without a strong technique when producers would comment to me that some of the actors I was bringing in for callbacks lacked levels to their work. The producers liked the actors' look and thought they were right for the role, but knew that they did not bring anything to the audition. The choices they made (or didn't make) lacked conviction. The lack of technique in these actors created an aura that they couldn't act. This wasn't the case, so this confused and frustrated me. I saw potential in these actors, and from my perspective auditioning is about showing potential. It is that potential that we as a production will take a chance on.

However, the producers need to see beyond the potential in the audition room. They need the confidence to know that this actor is going to be able to deliver a performance. In daytime television, that could mean twenty or thirty pages of dialogue, several days a week. The producers need to feel confident that the actor has enough technique to translate the potential he shows in the audition into solid, workable choices, every day in the television studio. Daytime television is also a business, and the program needs to feel confident in the investment it is making.

The producers need to feel confident that your acting training can be displayed in the audition room. I developed this technique because I knew that talented actors needed special skills in order to show their stuff in an audition situation. I have every confidence in this technique. I teach and discuss this technique whenever I am asked to speak to a group of actors, at colleges and theatres around the country and in New York at TVI Studios. The technique is designed to put you through a step-by-step process so that you can better understand the complete audition, not just your character. It encourages you to create a structure for success and allows you to experience that success while applying the technique. Let's start.

CHAPTER 11

Beats and
Beat Changes

The first thing you do once you get your sides is read the sides. Sound pretty simple? Next thing you do is break the scene into beats. What are beats? I mean, what really are the beats of a scene? If you have taken any acting class, enrolled in any Acting 101 in college, or performed in a play, you had some teacher or director somewhere say, "Break the scene down into beats." You nodded your head like you knew what the teacher was talking about, but you really didn't. This isn't your fault, though. You didn't know what it meant because no one ever thoroughly explained it to you. Well, now I will try. I have spent a lot time debating this with teachers and thinking about the best way to explain the beats. I have found through the workshops that I teach that the following explanation seems to stand up. While I know there are teachers who will disagree with me about the definition of a beat, from my perspective, given the kind of scenes the actors will be dealing with in auditions and in daytime television, this simple, straightforward definition is easy to use and extremely workable.

When the two characters in a scene are talking about, dealing with, or discussing a certain topic, then that is a beat about that topic. Until they stop dealing with that specific topic, it must be considered a beat about that topic. When one of the characters introduces a new subject, or changes the subject, that change is called a "beat change." While the characters are dealing with that new subject, that beat is about the new subject, until a new topic is introduced. In essence, when that happens, the beat has changed again. Clear?

Let me give an example. If a husband and wife in a scene are discussing the possibility of getting a divorce, while they are talking about the divorce, that is a beat about divorce. If the wife determines that she doesn't want to talk about the divorce anymore and wants to change the subject to their children, then she has changed the beat. The new beat will now be about their children.

Beat Changes Are in the Script

Now, something that is very important in understanding and determining the beats of a scene is to acknowledge that the beat changes are in the script. The beat changes are not about your character. What I mean by that is, your character in your audition does not always change the beat. Yes, your character can change a beat, but the other character in the audition scene can change the subject too. In essence, the writer has determined the beats; you just have to identify them. This is one of the few times in auditioning that I will stress that something is not always about you. However, this is done to assist you.

Write on Your Sides

Now, you are going to start writing on your sides. When you determine where the beat changes in the sides are, you indicate the change with a line in the right margin of your sides at the point where the topic has changed. You do this throughout your scene wherever a beat has changed. A warning about beats and beat changes: Keep it simple. Most actors agonize over this and put too many beats in their scenes. This will create confusion and cause a great deal of overthinking. If you are unsure whether a topic has changed between characters, you should leave it. I would much rather see an actor have longer and fewer beats than have many short beats. Below is an example of two characters dealing with a topic, then changing that topic. It is a simple setup to a scene to illustrate my point.

             MAN

    Are you hungry?

             WOMAN

    Yes. I'm hungry.

             MAN

    What do you want to eat?

Beats and Beat Changes ■ 53

```
                    WOMAN

I don't know.

                    MAN

Do you want Chinese food?

                    WOMAN

No.

                    MAN

Do you want Italian food?

                    WOMAN

I'm not in the mood for Italian food.

                    MAN

How about sushi?

                    WOMAN

I don't think I'm hungry after all. I think

I would rather go bowling. Do you want to go

bowling?
```

After you read this scene, you must determine what the characters are talking about. What is the topic they are dealing with? For the majority of this section, the characters are dealing with the topic of food and where they are going to have dinner. As long as the characters are talking about dinner/food/where to eat, the characters are still in that beat. In this scene, when the Woman introduces the topic of bowling, the beat changes. The easiest way to check yourself and your choices is to ask yourself, Does one line of dialogue have anything to do with the other? Does Chinese food have anything to do with being hungry and going to dinner? Yes, it does. Does Italian food? Yes, that does too; it's the same subject. How about bowling? Does bowling have anything to do with food? No, it doesn't. If it has nothing to do with the previously discussed topic, then the beat has changed. Subject changed, beat changed—so mark it in your script.

Now, the actual point where you should indicate this beat in the script is up for discussion and will be determined by the individual actor. The beat changes mark a change in subject, but it really marks a change in the characters' thoughts and feelings. The beat change is a moment where the actor takes a brief moment to change his thoughts so that he can change the subject. The beats and beat changes will determine the tempo of the audition. My personal suggestion would be to put the beat change after "I don't think I'm hungry after all" and before "I think I would rather go bowling." This way, in the playing of the scene, the actor can take a moment to change his thought before changing the topic and introduce the subject of bowling.

The acting component in this beat change will be for the actor to determine why the character is changing the subject. Is she not hungry? Does she love to go bowling? Actually, it could be connected to a larger choice that I will discuss in an upcoming chapter. While the characters are dealing with whether they will go bowling or not, that is a beat about bowling. When a character introduces another subject, you have another beat change, leading you into a full new beat. You once again mark the beat change in the right margin in your script.

                MAN

        Are you hungry?

                WOMAN

        Yes. I'm hungry.

                MAN

        What do you want to eat?

                WOMAN

        I don't know.

                MAN

        Do you want Chinese food?

                WOMAN

        No.

                MAN

        Do you want Italian food?

                    WOMAN

I'm not in the mood for Italian food.

                    MAN

How about sushi?

                    WOMAN

I don't think I'm hungry after all. I think

I would rather go bowling. Do you want to go

bowling?

                    MAN

Bowling? We haven't gone bowling in years.

                    WOMAN

I know that.

                    MAN

Then why do you want to go? Why would you

say you are not hungry and decide you want

to go bowling?

                    WOMAN

I don't know. Perhaps...perhaps...it

will be fun.

                    MAN

Well, I don't want to go bowling. Let's go

to Luigi's for dinner—it's our favorite

place.

So, the beat about bowling would go from the beat change as indicated all the way to, "Let's go to Luigi's for dinner. . ." As they continued to discuss bowling with the use of their dialogue, they are still in
that same beat. The Man questions her about why she would want to go
bowling; the Woman says it will be fun. They continue this short beat

until the subject of Luigi's is introduced. Once again, I would indicate the change before the previously mentioned line as so:

```
                    MAN
Well, I don't want to go bowling. Let's go

to Luigi's for dinner—it's our favorite

place.
```

I like the beat change to come before the new topic is introduced. It allows you to finish the previous topic before staring a new one. The character/actor changes the thought by taking a moment in the playing of the audition to think about the thought and have a feeling about the thought, then introduces the new information. Now, the beat about Luigi's will continue until a new topic is introduced. The scene would continue as follows:

```
                    MAN
Well, I don't want to go bowling. Let's go

to Luigi's for dinner—it's our favorite

place.
                    WOMAN
Luigi's. We haven't been there in years.

                    MAN
I know. That's why we should go.
```

                    WOMAN

The last time we were there—

                    MAN

I proposed to you.

                    WOMAN

That was so romantic. Luigi's is romantic.

                    MAN

We could use a little romance.

                    WOMAN

Yes.

                    MAN

We'll go?

                    WOMAN

No.

                    MAN

Yes or no?

                    WOMAN

No. I don't want to go. We can't go.

                    MAN

Why not?

                    WOMAN

Because I saw you and your girlfriend there!

I know you've been cheating on me.

As you can see, they continue to talk about Luigi's in this beat. It is not until the Woman introduces the girlfriend that different information is introduced. This would represent a beat change. I would suggest putting the beat change mark before "Because I saw you and your girl-friend there!" for the most dramatic effect, and to allow the actor to take a moment before introducing such a topic.

```
                WOMAN

    No. I don't want to go. We can't go.

                MAN

    Why not?

                WOMAN

    Because I saw you and your girlfriend there!

    I know you've been cheating on me.
```

Please note that there are three beat changes in this scene, and both characters initiate beat changes by introducing new topics to be discussed. So, if you were the man, you would only be changing one beat, and if you were the woman, you would be changing two beats. This is important, because as mentioned earlier, most actors think their character always changes the beat, and that is not always the case. This is important to recognize, because if you were audition-ing for the woman and approached the scene looking only for the beat changes that *you* introduce, you would be missing one beat change. You would also miss a moment where a shift of thoughts and feelings could be clearly expressed, as well as a transition in the storytelling.

Marking the beat changes accomplishes several objectives and establishes a framework for the scene for the actor to use during the audition. Many of these objectives will be made clear during the upcom-ing chapters, as all the stages of the technique are connected to each other. As I said earlier, a beat change marks an introduction of new information, a change in the topic to be discussed.

What does this do for you, the actor? It marks a change in your thoughts and feelings. When an actor or a character changes thoughts and feelings, he can actually take a second to actively acknowledge that has happened. What this does is help create the pace of the audition as well as allow you to achieve an objective. Consider the beat changes to be like the arm gate at a tollbooth. While driving your car on a highway, you will eventually pull up to a tollbooth. You don't actually stop the car fully as you toss some change into the bucket. Instead, you sort of slow down to a roll, as you wait for the arm gate to rise after it receives your payment.

The beat changes are just like those arm gates. You are driving the scene along, dealing with the topic of your dialogue, when the beat changes and a new topic is introduced, along with new feelings and thoughts. You take a second to acknowledge those new feelings and thoughts, and then you roll into the next beat. You don't completely stop your audition to think about the thoughts and feelings; you simply pause and roll so that the scene remains active. This is very important, as the beats determine the transitions between the sections of your audition piece. Below, I have included the full scene. Take a look at where the beat changes are.

MAN

Are you hungry?

WOMAN

Yes. I'm hungry.

MAN

What do you want to eat?

WOMAN

I don't know.

MAN

Do you want Chinese food?

WOMAN

No.

MAN

Do you want Italian food?

                    WOMAN

I'm not in the mood for Italian food.

                    MAN

How about sushi?

                    WOMAN

I don't think I'm hungry after all. I think

I would rather go bowling. Do you want to go

bowling?

                    MAN

Bowling? We haven't gone bowling in years.

                    WOMAN

I know that.

                    MAN

Then why do you want to go? Why would you

say you are not hungry and decide you want

to go bowling?

                    WOMAN

I don't know. Perhaps...perhaps...it

will be fun.

                    MAN

Well, I don't want to go bowling. Let's go

to Luigi's for dinner—it's our favorite

place.

                    WOMAN

Luigi's. We haven't been there in years.

                    MAN

I know. That's why we should go.

        WOMAN

The last time we were there—

        MAN

I proposed to you.

        WOMAN

That was so romantic. Luigi's is romantic.

        MAN

We could use a little romance.

        WOMAN

Yes.

        MAN

We'll go?

        WOMAN

No.

        MAN

Yes or no?

        WOMAN

No. I don't want to go. We can't go.

        MAN

Why not?

        WOMAN

Because I saw you and your girlfriend there!

I know you've been cheating on me.

        MAN

What?

        WOMAN

You heard me...I saw you with her. I've

known for some time.

```
        MAN

It is absolutely not what you think.

        WOMAN

Please don't insult me.

        MAN

I am not trying to—

        WOMAN

It actually feels good to finally confront

you about it, because I cannot live this lie

anymore.
```

The way the beat changes are marked right now, the actors would have four long sections of dialogue to handle, with three beat changes creating the transitional moments. The scene is simple. My choices, if I am the actor auditioning, are simple, and I now have a very clear map to use in my rehearsal time and to take into the room with me for my first audition for this role. It gives me structure and guidance, and indicates to me clear moments of thoughts and feelings in relation to the dialogue on the page. I am keeping my interpretation of the dialogue simple, and the beat changes give me structure to present myself as a thinking, feeling, and living being. That is, if your acting instrument can absorb it.

Don't Overthink the Beat Changes

Now I am going to give you an example of an actor who is thinking too much about the beats and is including many more beats than necessary. If you take the first beat—the one that deals with dinner and food—you could argue that every time a character introduces a new place to eat, it could be a beat change. If an actor wanted to make this choice, his sides might contain beat changes similar to those indicated below. In my opinion, this would only create a choppy and overanalyzed audition. This is not what I recommend, but rather an example of what *not* to do.

                    MAN

Are you hungry?

                    WOMAN

Yes. I'm hungry.

                    MAN

What do you want to eat?

                    WOMAN

I don't know.

                    MAN

Do you want Chinese food?

                    WOMAN

No.

                    MAN

Do you want Italian food?

                    WOMAN

I'm not in the mood for Italian food.

                    MAN

How about sushi?

                    WOMAN

I don't think I'm hungry after all. I think

I would rather go bowling. Do you want to go

bowling?

An actor could make a case that every time a new place to eat is introduced, more specific information about the topic is being discussed.
This may be true. However, if you realize that every time there is a change
in topic you are taking a split second to acknowledge your change in
thoughts, then in the above example, you will have three beat changes
on the same topic, rather than three beat changes for the entire audition
scene. That is a lot of thoughts, and a lot of transitional moments while

starting and stopping. This is not dramatic. These moments will take away from the pace of the scene. I will discuss this further in chapter 17, "Dictate the Pace". I prefer that you have longer beats on the same topic, rather than smaller beats that are specific to the same topic. Don't have sub-beats for your audition.

Specificity is a very important element in acting and auditioning. However, in my opinion, for beats it is better to deal with larger and broader areas on the topic. In this stage of the technique, simplicity should win out over specificity. Save the beat changes to answer the question of *why*. Why is my character changing the beat here? Why is the other character changing the subject? In my example, if you analyze the why in regard to every time a new ethnic style of food is proposed, you realize that it is not that interesting. The choice of changing the subject from dinner to bowling is perhaps masking some subtextual moment of the character's psyche and needs. A character is changing the subject for a reason.

During the live audition, you want the beat changes to be emotionally active moments. That activeness consists of the silent feelings you have about what you are about to say (if you change the beat) or the feelings about what you have just listened to (if the other character changes the beat). Once you have let that active emotional moment play out, you can move on to the next topic. You must then let that moment transform into the next stage of dialogue. I will refer back to this chapter and to how the beats are the base from which to work in implementing the technique.

CHAPTER 12

Major Beat Change

Now, you've read your sides. You've broken the sides into beats and have indicated all of your beat changes. You now have to determine what the major beat change is. The "major beat change" is the most important introduction of information in a scene. It is this information that has the greatest effect upon your character.

There is only one major beat change in an audition scene. It is your job to determine which beat change is the major beat change. There are two basic principles to determining the major beat change: (1) You must recognize that there is only one major beat change (not two or three; don't talk yourself into the option that there might be), and (2) It is completely up to you to decide where it is. Once again, there aren't any right or wrong answers, just choices. These are your choices. If the major beat change is the most important introduction of information, and as an actor you are aware of that moment in your text, then you can work to make it a viable, alive moment in your actual audition.

The major beat change is in a sense the greatest acting moment available to your character in the audition scene. It is the greatest acting moment because something major has been introduced or has occurred in the scene, and it has affected you either positively or negatively. It does not matter whether you introduced the topic or the other character did; it is the *effect* that we are looking for. If you can determine this moment for yourself, then you are giving yourself another preparation tool to get ready for a successful audition. It should be the clearest, most exciting, or most painful moment for you. It is the moment you can act like no other moment. If you can find this, you will have identified a wonderful nugget of information. Surprisingly, it is not that difficult to pinpoint.

Determining the Major Beat Change

The best way to determine what the major beat change is would be for you to analyze the level of importance of each beat change. So, looking at our scene, we have three beat changes. There is the beat change that introduces the subject of bowling, there is the beat change that introduces the subject of Luigi's restaurant, and there is the beat change that introduces the subject of the girlfriend and cheating.

You compare those subjects and the level of importance they all represent to each other and to your character. Is the introduction of bowling more important than the introduction of the subject of Luigi's? Maybe it is, maybe it's not. Perhaps Luigi's is more important because it has specific meaning to the characters. We learned from the scene that the characters were engaged there. Let's say Luigi's is more important. Is the introduction of the girlfriend more important than the introduction of Luigi's? You bet. In fact, it would be considered a major introduction of information. It greatly affects both characters, and that is why it would be labeled the major beat change. Most importantly, it affects your character directly.

Indicating the Major Beat Change

Now that you have determined this, what does this mean? What do you do? Well, you go back to your sides and you indicate on your beat change mark (which you have previously made) a symbol that shows you where the major beat change is. I suggest that you take that previously marked line and turn it into a big star or a big asterisk. Below, please look at what your new marked-up scene might look like now.

```
                MAN

        Are you hungry?

                WOMAN

        Yes. I'm hungry.

                MAN

        What do you want to eat?

                WOMAN

        I don't know.

                MAN

        Do you want Chinese food?
```

                WOMAN

No.

                MAN

Do you want Italian food?

                WOMAN

I'm not in the mood for Italian food.

                MAN

How about sushi?

                WOMAN

I don't think I'm hungry after all. I would

rather go bowling. Do you want to go

bowling?

                MAN

Bowling? We haven't gone bowling in years.

                WOMAN

I know that.

                MAN

Then why do you want to go? Why would you

say you are not hungry and decide you want

to go bowling?

                WOMAN

I don't know. Perhaps...perhaps...it will be

fun.

                MAN

Well, I don't want to go bowling. Let's go

to Luigi's for dinner—it's our favorite

place.

WOMAN

Luigi's. We haven't been there in years.

MAN

I know. That's why we should go.

WOMAN

The last time we were there—

MAN

I proposed to you.

WOMAN

That was so romantic. Luigi's is romantic.

MAN

We could use a little romance.

WOMAN

Yes.

MAN

We'll go?

WOMAN

No.

MAN

Yes or no?

WOMAN

No. I don't want to go. We can't go.

MAN

Why not?

WOMAN

Because I saw you and your girlfriend there!

I know you've been cheating on me.

```
          MAN
What?

          WOMAN
You heard me...I saw you with her. I've

known for some time.

          MAN
It is absolutely not what you think.

          WOMAN
Please don't insult me.

          MAN
I am not trying to—

          WOMAN
It actually feels good to finally confront

you about it, because I cannot live this lie

anymore.
```

Significance of the Major Beat Change

There are several significant reasons for locating the major beat change. The first, and most important, is how it affects the acting component. Typically, in the real world at my office, an audition would not be going well, when all of a sudden something special would happen. There would be a very clear moment that would stand out and grab my attention. This was usually a very subtle moment. However, in the subtleness of the moment, I would be moved, and the actor would suddenly be extremely focused. That moment would force me as a casting director to give that actor some notes and work with the scene again. That moment would give the actor another shot. Before that moment, the audition was average; the actor wasn't making choices. But that moment would give the actor another opportunity, even if he wasn't physically right for the role. I would mark in my notes that there was this one special moment that occurred. The moment would force me to remember the actor. I would recall writing in my notes, "not right here, but remember," or "something happened, bring back later." When I referred to those notes at a later date and saw that favorable information, it would remind me of the actor and give me confidence to have him come back for a new role. Remember, a first audition for a new role is technically a callback from a previous audition.

Now, those particular actors that this happened with didn't know this was the major beat change, and at the time, I didn't either. When I started developing the audition technique, I thought that there had to be some way to replicate this moment through technique. In a way, I was trying to pinpoint a spot for the actors to make that moment happen—to fill the moment with clear acting. Because that's what happened in my observation, I realized that, for that brief time, the actor was so connected to the scene that it became more alive than any other moment. So, I came up with the major beat change. If you are not physically right for the role, or if you are just not having the best audition, but you can fully understand, incorporate, and play the major beat change moment, then you will have at least one positive moment in an audition. That one positive acting moment will get you remembered. One positive audition moment is usually better than most actors auditioning for that role on that day. The major beat change is not to be used as a crutch, but I like to think of it as insurance policy; it is there for you if you need to rely on it.

One Crucial Moment

All the great characters in all the great plays have one crucial moment in the course of their lives that affects them more than any other moment. This moment creates conflict and causes them to take action. In the preparation of a play, it is vital for an actor to determine that moment. My thinking is that since that one crucial moment appears in plays, perhaps it can appear in television audition sides on a much smaller scale. The beauty of the major beat change is that it is clearly happening in the moment. This "now" is vital to the audition.

A hint: The major beat change usually occurs about three-quarters of the way through an audition scene.

The reason I suggest that it occurs about a three-quarters of the way through the scene is that, this way, enough dialogue has occurred before the major beat change is introduced to build up to it, and there is enough dialogue left in the scene to deal with the ramifications of the major beat change. In a three-page scene, if the major beat change was at the beginning, there would be too much time to deal with that information, and the scene would just become about that. None of the characters would want to move on to something new. If the major beat change appears too late in the scene, there is a lot of buildup to it, but there is no pay-off because the actor would not have sufficient time to deal with what has been introduced. So, look for the major beat change to occur about three-quarters of the way through a scene. This isn't a concrete rule—just good advice. Always make the most interesting choice that helps you in your audition.

The major beat change is also directly connected to the major objective. The major objective is another piece of the technique and will be discussed in its own chapter.

CHAPTER 13

Subject Word

Now that you've broken the scene into beats and have determined what the major beat change is, you now have to decide what the "subject word" is. This is not difficult. The subject word is a single word that will represent the subject the characters are dealing with in each individual beat. So, you must now reread the scene with the purpose of determining what the subject word is. This should be easy, since you broke the scene down into beats based on the change in subject matter, so you already have a sense of what the characters are talking about. Simply ask yourself, "What are the topics the characters are talking about?" "What are they dealing with?" If you look at our example scene, it is easy to determine that in the first beat, the characters are deciding whether they are hungry and where they are going to eat. In the second beat, they are talking about going bowling. The third beat is about Luigi's, and the fourth beat is about the affair.

Once you have clarified this, you pick one word that best connects with that topic/subject. This is your subject word. To be clear: You are looking at the full beat here, the topic that is being discussed in the beat, not necessarily the literal introduction of a word/topic that created the beat change. However, it is possible that your choice of a subject word could be the same word as the topic that determined there was a beat change. For example, "Luigi's" could be a subject word for the beat where 'Luigi's' was introduced at the very top of the beat change. In a way, determining the subject word is like playing a word association game. My hope is that the one specific word will trigger an association of the complete subject matter of the beat.

Example Subject Words

For example, in the first beat, the subject word could be "food." It could also be "restaurant"—it could even be "sushi." Any word that connects to that beat and what the characters are dealing with. My preference is the word "food." You can choose any word mentioned or come up with your own word. That is the point: this is for you to decide. The words should cover broad thoughts, but broad thoughts are just fine for the subject word and the first audition. In the second beat, my word would be "bowling." In the third beat, it could be either "engagement" or "Luigi's." The fourth subject word would be "affair." The point of the subject word is that it summarizes the beat's subject matter into one single word. This will be a helpful tool when preparing for the audition (On the Clock) and also when you are in the actual audition room. I will explain that in a moment.

Write the Subject Words Down

Once you've decided on your subject word, you write that word in the right margin space of your audition sides. You write this large enough to read. Below, please find what your audition scene might look like now, with the subject word and the beat changes indicated:

Are you hungry?

WOMAN

Food

Yes. I'm hungry.

MAN

What do you want to eat?

WOMAN

I don't know.

MAN

Do you want Chinese food?

WOMAN

No.

MAN

Do you want Italian food?

WOMAN

I'm not in the mood for Italian food.

                WOMAN

I'm not in the mood for Italian food.

        MAN

How about sushi?

        WOMAN

I don't think I'm hungry after all. I would

rather go bowling. Do you want to go bowling?

        MAN   *Bowling*

Bowling? We haven't gone bowling in years.

            WOMAN

I know that.

        MAN

Then why do you want to go? Why would you

say you are not hungry and decide you want

to go bowling?

        WOMAN

I don't know. Perhaps...perhaps...it

will be fun.

        MAN

Well, I don't want to go bowling. Let's go

to Luigi's for dinner—it's our favorite   *Luigi's*

place.

            WOMAN

Luigi's. We haven't been there in years.

        MAN

I know. That's why we should go.

            WOMAN

The last time we were there—

                    MAN

I proposed to you.

                    WOMAN

That was so romantic. Luigi's is romantic.

                    MAN

We could use a little romance.

                    WOMAN
Yes.

                    MAN

We'll go?

                    WOMAN

No.

                    MAN

Yes or no?

                    WOMAN

No. I don't want to go. We can't go.

                    MAN

Why not?

AFFAIR

                    WOMAN

Because I saw you and your girlfriend there!

I know you've been cheating on me.

                    MAN

What?

                    WOMAN

You heard me...I saw you with her. I've

known for some time.

MAN

It is absolutely not what you think.

WOMAN

Please don't insult me.

MAN

I am not trying to—

WOMAN

It actually feels good to finally confront

you about it, because I cannot live this lie

anymore.

A Reference Point

While preparing for the actual audition, you will now have a subject word to refer to right on your page. While you're working on the scene, you can actually just glance down at your subject word to help remind yourself of the actual subject matter that you are dealing with while you are getting comfortable with the dialogue. The more times you practice, the more comfortable you will become with using the word, and the more comfortable you will become dealing with the subject that your character is dealing with. The hope is that the repetition breeds familiarity. The word allows your mind to associate it with the topic of the beat; then you can let the dialogue assist you in the communication of the subject. Hopefully, the subject word is a safety net, and a signpost that will keep you focused on the dialogue. After practicing with this word for a significant period of time, if you find it does not create the familiarity and speed you desire, then change the word and try again.

CHAPTER 14

Feeling Word

Now that you have one subject word per beat, you must determine the "feeling word" per beat. What is the feeling word? Like the subject word, the feeling word is the word that gives you an association for the beat, but in this case, it states the overall emotions of the beat. It is the word that best describes the character's feelings on the subject during the beat. Once again, there are no right or wrong answers, just choices. I can't stress this enough. This is not a test or a scavenger hunt for the truth. Two actors auditioning for the same part and using the same sides would most likely have different subject and feeling words—that is, of course, if they are using this technique. Everyone's choices will make his work individualized and specific, and that is why no two auditions are exactly the same.

The wonderful aspect of the feeling word is that you have a lot of flexibility to change it while you are practicing. The feeling word is the actual feeling that you will incorporate and embody during your audition. In our scene, you have three different beats, so you will have three different feeling words, which gives you three levels of feeling to play with. Other techniques ask actors to put a feeling word on every line. To me, this is too much to play. By picking one level of feeling per beat, you will actually stimulate more natural levels of feeling that will emerge through the use of the dialogue. The feeling word is the diving board for you to start the beat with; then you can allow other natural feelings to occur. While you are On the Clock, you can try different feeling words per beat to see what occurs. You decide what word best represents the feeling of your character when dealing with the given subject in the beat. It is certainly not the *only* feeling you will have during that beat, but the generic feeling. The thinking is that when you practice with the overall feeling, it will help you determine the specificity of the smaller moments in the beat. If the smaller specific feelings are completely different from the feeling word, then you may have to reexamine your beats and beat changes. I would venture to say that if you are feeling something completely different from your feeling word, then you are probably in a new beat, dealing with a new topic.

Determining the Feeling Words

In our scene, we have determined that the first subject word is "food." When determining the feeling word, ask, "How does my character feel overall about the subject in that beat?" If I am the Man, I could justify that I feel "angry" in the first beat because the Woman is being indecisive about where she wants to eat or what she wants to eat. This could make my character angry. Since it is your choice, you can even go the opposite way. You can determine that the Man is "happy." Perhaps he is happy because he is very hungry and he knows that soon he will be eating. Or, since he is very concerned about eating and since they are dealing with the subject word of "food," it makes him happy. Maybe he is "frustrated" because he is very hungry, and being hungry has put him in a bad mood because they cannot decide where to eat. If that is the word the actor chooses, he could start the scene being frustrated about the subject "food." Do you see how all of these technique elements connect so far? Everything is related. You must be clear about your subject word to determine your feeling word.

Justify Your Choices

The key to this is that you must be able to justify your choices. All of the examples given are playable words. Every actor has the ability to play the feelings of being angry, frustrated, or happy. To reiterate, the actors wouldn't necessarily play being happy for the entire beat, because the dialogue may not support those feelings, but you certainly can start being happy at the beginning of the beat, and let the feeling of being happy slowly dissipate as you realize there is indecision in determining what restaurant you may attend. The feeling word gives you a wonderful blanket of emotion to put over a beat, to help you when you practice and to give you guidance when you are in the audition room. I think it would even be safe for a first audition to just rely on the feeling word to dictate the feeling of each beat, and to let other natural feelings emerge at the audition. Then, if you are lucky enough to get a callback, when you are back On the Clock, you can get more specific with the levels of the feeling word for the beat. A reminder: If you get to the call-back, you are doing something right, so don't change your feeling word—just get more specific with it. Remember, polish your red car, don't paint it blue.

An Example: Justification

If I were the Woman in the scene, I might decide my feeling word is "annoyed" because I might feel annoyed that the Man keeps asking me where I want to eat, when I don't want to go eat dinner anyway. So, each character has different feeling words for the same subject. As an actor, you always want to pick feeling words that are active. Inactive words are harder to make playable. If you choose words such as "apathetic" or "numb," you run the risk of being stuck in those feelings and having a passive reading. Active words such as "angry" or "happy" can complement the dialogue and be used in conjunction with the major objective (which will be explained in chapter 16). The active feeling word is playable. You want to be able to take the word and drive the scene through the beat with active feeling. You imbue every line of dialogue with that feeling word.

A quick note about the scene that I have written for this book: It is a very simple scene, written this way so I can make my points about my technique very clear. I will always try to give examples of both characters in the scene making choices with the technique, but the truth is that a real audition scene is written heavily in favor of the role that needs to be cast, and usually the second character does not have as many choices to make.

Example: Feeling Words for the Man in the Scene

Getting back to the scene, let's take the perspective of an actor auditioning for the Man. If I were the Man, I would choose "angry" for the feeling word in the first beat about the subject word, "food." The second feeling word would be "annoyed," because I am annoyed that the woman wants to go "bowling" (subject word for beat number two). My next feeling word would be "excited," for the beat about "Luigi's." The Man would be excited to go to Luigi's because of the personal memories he has about that subject. The feeling word in the last beat would be "devastated." The Man would be or feel devastated because of the introduction of the major beat change, which is the subject word about the "affair." You should indicate the feeling words below the subject words on the sides. The Man's sides may look something like this:

MAN

Are you hungry?

Food

WOMAN

Yes. I'm hungry.

Angry

MAN

What do you want to eat?

WOMAN

I don't know.

MAN

Do you want Chinese food?

WOMAN

No.

MAN

Do you want Italian food?

WOMAN

I'm not in the mood for Italian food.

MAN

How about sushi?

WOMAN

I don't think I'm hungry after all. I would
rather go bowling. Do you want to go bowling?

Bowling

MAN

Annoyed

Bowling? We haven't gone bowling in years.

                WOMAN

I know that.

                MAN

Then why do you want to go? Why would you

say you are not hungry and decide you want

to go bowling?

                WOMAN

I don't know. Perhaps...perhaps...it

will be fun.

                MAN

Well, I don't want to go bowling. Let's go

to Luigi's for dinner—it's our favorite   *Luigi's*

place.

                WOMAN

Luigi's. We haven't been there in years.   *Excited*

                MAN

I know. That's why we should go.

                WOMAN

The last time we were there—

                MAN

I proposed to you.

                WOMAN

That was so romantic. Luigi's is romantic.

                MAN

We could use a little romance.

                WOMAN

Yes.

                    MAN

We'll go?

                    WOMAN

No.

                    MAN

Yes or no?

                    WOMAN

No. I don't want to go. We can't go.

                    MAN

Why not?

                    WOMAN

Because I saw you and your girlfriend there!

I know you've been cheating on me.

                    MAN
What?

                    WOMAN

You heard me...I saw you with her. I've

known for some time.

                    MAN

It is absolutely not what you think.

                    WOMAN

Please don't insult me.

                    MAN

I am not trying to—

                    WOMAN
It actually feels good to finally confront

you about it, because I cannot live this lie

anymore.

*AFFAIR
DEVASTATED*

A note of caution: Be careful not to have too much of a drastic change between one feeling word to the next. You want to be able to make clear, progressive, and subtle changes through the beat changes. You want to be true to your feelings for the beats, but if the feeling words are too drastically different, there will be too much jumping around in the playing of the scene. You don't want to come across as an emotional yo-yo who is psychotic and choppy. Remember, the beat change silence is filled with you thinking about what is being said, the new topic introduced, and how you feel about it all. It is there that you silently embody the feeling word and relate it to the new subject introduced. If it is a drastic change from the previous beat, then you must be able to justify it in your preparation in accordance with the new subject (beat change) and the subject word.

Example: Feeling Words for the Woman in the Scene

If I were the Woman in the scene, I would choose "annoyed" for the first beat. The second feeling word would be "hopeful," because I am hopeful that the Man wants to go "bowling" (subject word for beat number two) and that it will be fun for us. My feeling word for the next beat would be "insulted" for the beat about "Luigi's." The Woman would be insulted to talk about Luigi's because that is where she caught him having the affair. Feeling insulted would allow her to make an easy transition from this beat to the next beat, where she needs to feel confident. So, the feeling word in the last beat would be "confident." The Woman would feel or be confident that she has to make the introduction of the major beat change, which is the subject word about the "affair." This is what she has wanted to deal with. The Woman's sides would look like this:

                    MAN   *Food*

              Are you hungry?

                    WOMAN   *Annoyed*

              Yes. I'm hungry.

                    MAN

              What do you want to eat?

                    WOMAN

I don't know.

                    MAN

Do you want Chinese food?

                    WOMAN

No.

                    MAN

Do you want Italian food?

                    WOMAN

I'm not in the mood for Italian food.

                    MAN

How about sushi?

                    WOMAN

I don't think I'm hungry after all. I would

rather go bowling. Do you want to go bowling?   *Bowli*

                MAN   *Hopeful*

Bowling? We haven't gone bowling in years.

                WOMAN

I know that.

                MAN

Then why do you want to go? Why would you

say you are not hungry and decide you want

to go bowling?

                    WOMAN

I don't know. Perhaps...perhaps...it

will be fun.

                    MAN

Well, I don't want to go bowling. Let's go

to Luigi's for dinner—it's our favorite   *Luigi's*

place.

                    WOMAN   *INSULTED*

Luigi's. We haven't been there in years.

                    MAN

I know. That's why we should go.

                    WOMAN

The last time we were there—

                    MAN

I proposed to you.

                    WOMAN

That was so romantic. Luigi's is romantic.

                    MAN

We could use a little romance.

                    WOMAN

Yes.

                    MAN

We'll go?

                    WOMAN

No.

                    MAN

Yes or no?

                    WOMAN

No. I don't want to go. We can't go.

                    MAN

Why not?

                    WOMAN

Because I saw you and your girlfriend there!

I know you've been cheating on me.

AFFAIR

CONFIDENT

                    MAN

What?

                    WOMAN

You heard me...I saw you with her. I've

known for some time.

                    MAN

It is absolutely not what you think.

                    WOMAN

Please don't insult me.

                    MAN

I am not trying to—

                    WOMAN

It actually feels good to finally confront

you about it, because I cannot live this lie

anymore.

Now, don't ask yourself, "What if I am the actress making these choices, and the actor playing the Man doesn't make the same choices?" Don't worry about this, because as I mentioned earlier, auditioning is not a scene. There is no actor playing the Man; there is only a reader, going off whatever choices you have made. I am only showing you both characters to highlight for both sexes what different choices can be made.

Variations to Your Choices

To prove my point about the variations each actor can bring to an audition using the same sides, I will now give an example of the scene from the actress's perspective, by changing the subject and feeling words in each beat. In beat number one, I am going to change the subject word from "food" to "restaurants," and the feeling word from "annoyed" to "confused." My justification is that I am simply confused as to where I want to eat. I will change the subject word in beat number two from "bowling" to "sport," and the feeling word from "hopeful" to "fun." My justification of the feeling word is that it will be fun to play a sport with the Man, so I will play that beat in a fun manner. In the third beat, I will change the subject word from "Luigi's" to "café," and the feeling word from "insulted" to "angry." My justification is that she is angry because of the associations she now makes with that café and displays those feelings while talking about them in that beat. In the fourth beat, I will change the subject word from "affair" to "adultery," and the feeling word from "confident" to "nervous." My justification for the feeling word is that she is very nervous about bringing up the subject of adultery with the Man.

MAN

Are you hungry?

WOMAN

Yes. I'm hungry.

MAN

What do you want to eat?

WOMAN

I don't know.

MAN

Do you want Chinese food?

WOMAN

No.

MAN

Do you want Italian food?

RESTAURANTS

CONFUSED

                    WOMAN

I'm not in the mood for Italian food.

                    MAN

How about sushi?

                    WOMAN

I don't think I'm hungry after all. I would

rather go bowling. Do you want to go

bowling?

                    MAN

Bowling? We haven't gone bowling in years.

                    WOMAN   *Sport*

I know that.   *Fun*

                    MAN

Then why do you want to go? Why would you

say you are not hungry and decide you want

to go bowling?

                    WOMAN

I don't know. Perhaps...perhaps...it

will be fun.

                    MAN

Well, I don't want to go bowling. Let's go *Cafe*

to Luigi's for dinner—it's our favorite

place.

                    WOMAN   *Angry*

Luigi's. We haven't been there in years.

                    MAN

I know. That's why we should go.

                WOMAN

The last time we were there—

                MAN

I proposed to you.

                WOMAN

That was so romantic. Luigi's is romantic.

                MAN

We could use a little romance.

                WOMAN

Yes.

                MAN

We'll go?

                WOMAN

No.

                MAN

Yes or no?

                WOMAN

No. I don't want to go. We can't go.

                MAN

Why not?

                WOMAN

Because I saw you and your girlfriend there!
I know you've been cheating on me.

                MAN

What?

Adultery

Nervous

                    WOMAN

You heard me...I saw you with her. I've

known for some time.

                    MAN

It is absolutely not what you think.

                    WOMAN

Please don't insult me.

                    MAN

I am not trying to—

                    WOMAN

It actually feels good to finally confront

you about it, because I cannot live this lie

anymore.

My only justification for the words I choose is my own ability to convince myself that it is a playable choice that works within the context of the scene and in tandem with the dialogue that is written. All choices are valid choices if they do not seem obtrusive to the writer's intentions. This is what creates variety in every actor's audition.

No Indecisive Feelings

What I really like about the activeness of the feeling word is that it forces you to play some decisive feelings. By finding the word that works best for you, you force yourself not to play anything nonchalant or middle-of-the-road. You cannot go into an audition with the attitude that your character does not know how she feels about the subject in any given beat. The technique forces you to make choices; once you absorb those choices, you have something to do, and feel, and be. You are not in the audition to display ambivalent feelings. This is not reality; it is an audition. You will be much more interesting to watch if you decide how your character feels and play those feelings rather than being unsure about how your character feels and playing uncertainty.

CHAPTER 15

Summary (So Far)

If you look at my sides, they are completely written on and marked up. This is certainly done on purpose, with many objectives. What I am trying to create is a work-study sheet, perhaps even a cheat sheet—the CliffsNotes of auditioning. My sides now tell me how I, as an actor, should act when auditioning for this role. I know this just by looking at my sides. I have subject words that tell me what I am talking about in every beat. I have feeling words that tell me how I feel in every beat. I know I have three beat changes, four beats, and one major beat change, leaving me with four subject words and four feeling words. The major beat change highlights the most important information for my character. When I am rehearsing, I will use all of the words and lines, and my one asterisk, to guide me through the audition and allow me to incorporate the dialogue, bringing the audition to life.

Notes to the Test Are on Your Sides

There is an ulterior motive here. Let me tell you a story of how most first auditions go. You are told to come to my office at noon on a Friday. You work on your scene, making choices along the way. You feel prepared and slightly nervous, but you are looking forward to the opportunity. Friday arrives and you're running late. The subway, the traffic, you slept late . . . you get my point. You arrive, you sign in, and you take a seat. You sit in the waiting room and review your choices. Finally, I come to get you. I say hello, you follow me to my office. You nerves build as we walk down the hall. I ask you where you are from, and you answer. Next thing you know, I am asking if you have any questions or if you want to sit or stand for the reading. You're sitting, so you decide to stay in the security of the chair. I have the first line, so I start reading with you. You say your lines, you forget to take a breath, you start to sweat, you forget your choices, and the next thing you know, you are walking out of the building. The audition is over, and you don't even remember what happened. I am overdramatizing this to make my point, but it does happen.

Now, imagine the same scenario as the one above, but as I start my first line, you glance down at your sides, which are completely written on. Out of the corner of your eye, you see the words "food" and "angry." You have made such good use of your On the Clock time that when you see those words, something clicks. Something kicks in. Your body, your acting instrument, remembers that your character is angry (feeling word) because you can't decide what kind of food (subject word) you and your wife are going to eat. Take a breath, breathe in the feeling word, feel the feeling of the word, acknowledge the subject word, and go. You are on your way. Congratulations—you have been allowed to bring your notes to the test! Your homework pays off, and your choices and notes allow you to launch the audition with your choices. This is a great safety net if nerves come into play, and, let's face it—auditioning is nerve-racking.

CHAPTER 16

Major Objective

Now that you have the beats broken down, and you've chosen the subject and feeling words, and you've found the major beat change, you must now determine the major objective. The major objective is simple and vital to a successful audition. The major objective is what your character wants to achieve from the audition scene. It is what your character determines she wants before the scene starts. The major objective is the thing that propels the character's journey. That objective and that need to achieve something is what drives the scene. Now, I use the word "major" on purpose. This is because the major objective connects directly to the major beat change.

Major Objective and Major Beat Change Are Connected

The major beat change is the introduction of the most important information in the scene. The major objective is of equal importance. Knowing this will help you create a wonderful acting moment at the major beat change. The major beat change is the moment where the character either achieves or does not achieve her major objective.

I mentioned earlier that the major beat change was the place where the information that most affects your character is introduced. It would stand to reason that, if this information is that important, it is something that your character wanted and either got or did not get at that particular moment. What you want overall from the scene is your major objective. Whether you achieve your major objective or not at the major beat change is irrelevant. Either outcome creates wonderful acting opportunities. If you are successful in achieving your major objective at the major beat change, then that moment becomes about feeling that success. If you do not achieve your major objective at the major beat change, then that moment is about showing the disappointment of not achieving it.

Take Action

The major objective is about taking action. Your character is in pain and wants to relieve herself of that pain. She wants to achieve something, so she takes action to achieve what she wants. Without a major objective, there is no action. An actionless audition is passive. Passive auditions are boring. Boring auditions get lost in the large amount of actors auditioning; they don't stand out.

Using our scene, we have determined that the major beat change is the moment where the affair is introduced. So, if I were auditioning for the role of the Woman, an example of a major objective would be the Woman's need to confront her husband about his affair. This is the major event that the character needs to achieve in her life (to relieve the pain she is living with). The major beat change is the moment in the scene where that action is achieved. It is the moment where the character realizes that she has achieved her major objective or that she did not achieve her major objective. The major objective gives the character purpose and the major beat change gives her a great moment of realization. It is conceivable that the Woman in the scene has tried many times to confront her husband about the affair, but has never been able to do so. This scene would represent the moment when she gets to achieve success. In essence, the character's pain is so great that it demands attention, which translates into the major objective.

If I were auditioning for the Man in the scene, with the major beat change still being the introduction of the affair, my choice for a major objective would be for him to want to have a wonderful night of romance with his wife. In essence, he is trying to have another "normal" night and keep the secret about the affair. At the moment of the major beat change, the husband realizes that there is no romance, and he is not going to achieve his major objective. If you check back, the feeling word for that beat is "devastated." He got caught and did not achieve the major objective, so he is devastated because of that and the ramifications associated with it.

Another simple choice for the major objective would be to not get caught in the affair tonight. Since the actor knows that he *does* get caught, but the character does not, the actor can prepare for the spontaneous reaction to that information. In essence, the character will discover that he did not achieve his major objective. The *character* failed to achieve what he wanted, yet the *actor* can use his understanding of the scene to create a truthful and dynamic moment.

Look at the major beat change and work backward. Since I know what the major beat change is, I ask myself, "What could I choose to try to achieve that I know will be unsuccessful?" This will only work from the Man's point of view in this scene. If the actress makes a choice that her major objective is anything other than something to do with the major beat change (the affair), she will be setting up an unobtainable and uninteresting expectation. The actress should make the simple choice to use that information to clarify her major objective. As actors, you must always make the best available choices for your character. This is not a boring choice, but rather an immediate one.

The order of this technique asks you to make choices for all the previous steps, then, to determine the major objective, ask yourself, "What does my character want overall from the scene?" There is a reason I explain the technique in this order. It is imperative that you do the previous steps before trying to discover the major objective. The previous determination of the major beat change will help you determine the major objective. If you know what the most important introduction of information is, then you can ask what you can want in relation to that information.

If you are auditioning for the Woman and the major beat change occurs when your character introduces the affair, then the major objective can simply be that she wants to confront him about the affair, because she cannot live her life like this anymore. However, merely choosing to introduce the subject of the affair is not an interesting enough objective, so you must phrase the objective in a way that is more specific and makes your character stronger. Do this by making the objective about you (the Woman) and what you want from the moment: "My character's major objective is to confront her husband about his affair tonight, so that she can either fix her marriage or walk away from it." That is something that is achievable through the scene, and you can justify it based on the dialogue. In her last line of the scene, she states that she cannot live with the lie of an affair anymore. It is easy to think that she has resolved this objective by the end of the scene, or is at least on her way to resolution.

The Major Objective is about What You Want for You

You never want to make your objective about trying to make the other person do something. I realize that many of you may have been taught in your acting classes that your actions and objectives should achieve an effect on your partner, but this is not an acting class or a rehearsal. This is your television audition. This is a frequent mistake amongst auditioners. If I were auditioning for the Woman, a terrible major objective for the sides would be to try to get the Man to apologize for the affair or to make him feel bad about it. That may very well be a justified reaction or need in the real world, but this is not the real world—this is a television audition. The Man in the scene is a reader, and you know by reading the sides that he does not apologize for his actions, so by striving for that as your major objective, you are chasing something that is never going to be achieved. If you have a chance to achieve something or get a hint of success, then it is always best to make that positive effort to do that. The Man's character may indeed apologize in a later episode, but you should only be concerned about the now. When I work with students on this technique, many of their responses are about getting the other character to do something. I remind them that this is not a scene and that they need to be concerned with what they want. This is another way of empowering you. Remember, it is your audition; make it about you.

Major Objective Creates a Natural Level of Subtext

This is a little advanced, but I am going to write it here anyway. An additional benefit to the major objective is that it creates a natural level of subtext. If the Woman acknowledges that her major objective is to confront her husband, then all of the beats will be flavored with that understanding. For example, the Man wants to go to dinner and his wife does not. Perhaps she does not want to go to dinner because she feels she may not be able to achieve her major objective at dinner (confronting him). She suggests going bowling. Perhaps if they go bowling, she will have a better opportunity to achieve her major objective in that environment, because it will be relaxing and she can catch him off guard. When the beat changes to Luigi's restaurant, the pain is so great, the feelings are so uncomfortable (since that is where she saw him cheating), that she finally takes action and the major beat change occurs. She introduces the topic of the affair and she, at long last, has achieved her major objective.

Bring in the feeling word in that beat, and you can make a case that the "insulted" feelings created by that beat have forced her to recognize her pain. These feelings have also given her the confidence to take action through changing the subject and introducing the major beat change.

The reverse could be said for the Man. Perhaps his major objective is to rekindle his marriage, or to not get caught tonight. All of his actions in the scene are to avoid the topic of the affair. When the Woman introduces the major beat change, in that moment, the Man does not achieve his major objective. The major beat change creates great acting opportunities for both roles. Also, you now have a complete audition scene with a drive and a purpose.

The natural subtext arrives because the characters are thinking about their major objective; they are trying to achieve their major objective while they are using the dialogue that may not connect directly to their major objective, but their major objective is always on their mind, so it flavors their perspective on the scene. This creates levels of feeling. However, I must warn you: It is always imperative that you play what is happening in the beat you are in, and let the natural subtext be just that—natural.

Keep It Simple

The trick to the major objective is to realize the answers are in the script. You just have to find the right questions. Since the major beat change and the major objective are connected, and you have already determined what the major beat change is, just ask yourself, What could my character want, based on the major beat change moment? Keep it simple and direct. Do not make it complicated by including things that are not in the script. If, while preparing an audition for either of these characters, you decide that the major objective is to buy a car, or to get the other to apologize or say, "I love you," then you've chosen something that is really not in the script. It is in your head. We can't see what is in your head. My thinking? Do what is in the script—only, do it very well. Many actors suggest that you need to make big, interesting choices to stand out. I disagree. When actors think and work that way, their choices appear odd or at the very least misplaced. The audition comes across like an actor trying to make something out of something that is not there. I say, take what is on the page and do it very specifically and very well. This is directly related to daytime television. Most actors do not do the little things well.

Positive Result

One of the residual results of the major objective is that it takes away any indecisiveness you have as an actor and also as character. Actors will tell me in my office and in class that, in life, they often do not know what they want in a given situation, so they make the choice to play a character in an audition scene as if the character does not know what he wants from the other person. This may very well be acceptable in real life, but auditioning is not reflective of real life. It is what it is—an audition. The major objective forces you to make a decision about what you want for your character, not what you want from the other character. It doesn't allow you to play ambivalence—hoping to discover what you want. Just as the feeling word makes you feel the feelings in the scene, the major objective forces you to try to achieve something. It launches you on a journey.

Remind Yourself of the Major Objective before You Begin

The major objective is a wonderful preparation tool for the actual audition. When you are in the waiting room, or right before you start your audition, you should remind yourself of what your major objective is. If you remind yourself of what your major objective is, and then see your first subject word and feeling word, you will be ready to start your audition. If you have fully embodied your choices when you were rehearsing, then they will come back to you the moment before you start reading.

Don't Forget to Be an Actor

I do not want to contradict anything I have said up to this point in the book; I just want to make sure that I am not making an assumption either. I am assuming that you will not forget to act. As actors, you must accept and play that there is a relationship between the two people, there are feelings and desires and objectives. You, the actor, must bring your own sensitivity to the work. You must accept that the technique and the acting must be a blending of skills that will be evident to a casting director. That blending is what makes the audition unique to you. An audition is never just about the technique, and it is never just feelings or acting. The audition is about all of those things. Give yourself permission to be creative in using the technique as a framework. So, even though I stress to play what is on the page, allow yourself to be affected by how the information on the page affects your character and your character's major objective.

CHAPTER 17

Dictate the Pace

As an actor, you believe that you are powerless and helpless when you enter the audition room. However, there is a very simple way for you to empower yourself, and that is through the pacing of the scene. Yes, you are powerless to make decisions for the decision-makers, but you can control two key factors. One, you can control the On the Clock time—your own discipline to prepare—and two, you can dictate the pace of the actual audition. From the moment the casting director says, "Whenever you are ready, please begin," you have a tremendous amount of power. The moment the audition scene is over, you are rendered powerless again.

Wouldn't you like to be able to control what is controllable? Ironically, most actors I meet give up that power during their audition. They forfeit it over to the reader by allowing him to dictate the pace of the scene. You can make all the acting choices you want, but if you do not display them in a passionate way, they will not stand out. By dictating the pace of the reading, by having a character who passionately and energetically wants to achieve something, you have a better opportunity to stand out.

How do you do this? It is easy. You use your major objective. We now know that the major objective is what your character wants from the scene, so embody that need with passion and energy to try to achieve it. You do this most clearly by driving the major objective to all of the beat changes. Drive to one beat change, listen and react, drive to the next beat change, listen and react, and so on. Let each new subject and your feelings and thoughts for that subject determine when you start the new beat. In that moment, you must also relate it to your major objective, creating natural subtext. The beat changes may be absent of dialogue, but they are filled with emotional thoughts of transitions. That is the acting answer for how to dictate the scene's pace.

Pick up Your Cues

A technical answer to how to dictate the scene's pace would be that you must drive the scene by picking up your cues. Don't allow a significant amount of dead air between the reader's line and your own. A great metaphor for this is "playing catch" with the reader. This is a basic acting exercise done in most beginning acting classes, where the person who has the first line in the scene begins with a ball in her hand. When she says her line, she tosses the ball to her scene partner. The same game can be utilized in an audition, in a metaphorical way.

The key to controlling the pace of the scene is to make in-the-moment adjustments off of the reader. For example, if the reader is reading more slowly than you desire, throw the ball back right away ("tight cue" your lines). If the reader is tight cueing her lines and you would like to pace the scene with a little more time for transitions, hold on to your line a moment longer before tossing it back to her. If you are solid in your technique, you can make these in-the-room adjustments.

Don't Blame the Reader

The hope is that the reader will follow your lead. If the reader is a good reader or casting director, then she will instinctively do this. If she is not, you will have to work harder in the actual reading, but can still accomplish this goal. I promise you that it will be different from your preparation at home, but that is why I stressed earlier that this is an audition and not a performance. You cannot possibly know in advance the tempo that the reader will take on. So, don't leave yourself open to that vulnerability. If by the end of the scene you feel like the tempo of the audition was off, trust that what the casting director is observing about you is your purpose and effort. If that is the impression that you leave behind in the room, then that purpose and effort will be two things more than the actor before you, who just went with the flow of the reader. To me, that kind of audition comes across as passionless.

Often when I am teaching, students tell me that their audition didn't feel right, or that it wasn't what they had planned because the reader threw them off. I say that is an excuse. Never blame the reader—blame yourself. Auditions are important, and if you put all of your trust into an intern, or an assistant, or a casting director, or even another actor who is serving as a reader, to help guide you through your audition, then you did not accept responsibility for this audition and should only blame yourself.

Caution: Dictating the pace is not the same thing as speeding. A fast audition is meaningless. You must allow the major objective to be the guide for you. It is the bus that you drive through the scene, sometimes moving faster than at other times, based on your beat changes. Speed for the sake of speed is just a fast audition without purpose or levels. You should be a shark, constantly in motion, looking to eat up the dialogue that is coming at you and that you are saying. Be aggressive like a shark. There—a few more metaphors for you.

Empower yourself. You are an important actor. You must be better than all the people in front of you and better than every actor that walks into the casting director's office after you. Stand out and take control!

CHAPTER 18

Think and Feel on the Lines

This chapter should really be called "Think and Feel on the Lines, Not Around Them". This is because the *around* part is the trap that the most actors fall into. To clarify: The things I want you to concentrate on are thinking about what the other character is saying to you, expressing feelings about what is being said, and reacting to what is being said while saying your lines to the reader. The key to this is tempo. This is a wonderful accompaniment to "Dictate the Pace". The ability to think and feel on the lines will allow you to keep an aggressive tempo and control the pace of the scene.

Don't Anticipate

The key to thinking and feeling on the lines is to not rush your response and to not anticipate the reader's lines coming toward you. You want to keep the energy up, but not at the expense of the scene going stale. You want to actively and emotionally keep the energy in line with listening and responding. The metaphorical ball that you are playing catch with is juggled for the split second that you are listening, then tossed back on your reaction. Listen, react. Listen, feel, and react. Listen, feel, react, and speak.

Don't listen . . . think about what is said . . . think about feeling . . . feel feelings . . . show feelings . . . speak. Imagine if that were done for the majority of your cues; the scene would lack any sense of pace. It would be too slow. Not dramatic, but slow. Without a sense of pace, the scene is not alive. If the scene is not alive, then your character does not want anything. If your character does not want anything, you have no major objective. You must trust the dialogue that the writer has given you. Without a major objective, you have no reason for being there. Every aspect of this technique is connected to every other aspect.

Use the Beat Changes

The moments where you can take a bit longer to think and feel before reacting are at the beat changes. As mentioned earlier, the beat changes are like gates at a tollbooth. Let the moment actively pass, then react to the new topic that was introduced or change the subject yourself, if that is how the scene is written. The major beat change would represent the longest active pause, the deepest place of thoughts and feelings without dialogue. This would be the most important exchange of information in the scene, so your character needs that much longer to absorb what has happened or what she is about to do. Keep the ball in the air, but keep it *alive* in the air, thinking and feeling and breathing.

CHAPTER 19

Avoid Subtext

There is a place for subtext in an audition, but I believe that actors need to be careful of overusing it. Because I am fearful of overuse, my advice for all actors is to avoid subtext during their first audition for a specific role. In the chapter about the major objective, I explained that one of the advantages of the major objective is that it creates a natural level of subtext. However, that subtext is directly related to what the character wants, and its use is subtle. Sometimes even the actor himself is unconscious that subtext is showing, because he is just playing his major objective. To be clear: Subtext is when your character is *saying* one thing and *feeling* another, or when your character is *thinking* one thing and *saying* another. It's when opposite or contrasting feelings are being expressed. Subtext is very present in daytime television and the daytime audition. A character looks at another and tells him that she hates him, but underneath it is clear that she has positive feelings for him.

It has been my experience that actors love to use subtext in their auditions and in their actual work. However, subtext for the sake of subtext is not interesting enough. If it is an accompaniment to the major objective, then it creates a level of feeling and thought for the actors to play with their objectives. The subtext should be directly connected to the character's wants and needs. Subtext is like quicksand. If you rely on it, you will get stuck in it, you will begin to sink in it, you will be unable to get yourself out of the trap. If you cannot get out, you cannot progress, and you cannot move forward. An audition that does not move forward lacks a major objective, desire, and passion. You can have desire and passion, but if you get stuck in the subtextual quicksand, it will overwhelm your understanding of an objective and not allow you to move forward.

So, for a first audition, my advice is to avoid the use of the subtext. Don't let it get in the way of the activeness of an audition. It will naturally be there as you strive to achieve the major objective and certainly can start to be added into your auditions as you get to the callback and screen test stages.

To clarify: The use of subtextual feelings on specific lines is not a good choice for a first audition. In our scene, the Woman's major objective could be to confront her husband about the affair. When the Man wants to go out to dinner, for a split second, the actress might think about how that will affect her objective; however, the real, honest playing of that beat must still be about the issue of food, and what the couple will eat for dinner. How the food discussion affects her major objective is strictly an additional benefit. So, that's an example of allowing subtext to assist in a beat in a positive manner.

Negative Use of Subtext

The trap that most actors will fall into with the use of subtext is on specific lines. In beat number one, the Woman has a line that reads, "I am not in the mood for Italian food." That is a simple line in response to a direct question asked by the Man: "Do you want Italian food?" Actors should always play the literal meaning of the line and no more. When the Woman responds, "I am not in the mood for Italian food," it is an honest evaluation of her hunger. It should not be interpreted as a loaded, subtextual moment, played for the sake of being dramatic. If you are auditioning for the Woman and you get to the later stages of this audition, you can flavor that line a bit, perhaps, but I urge you to think about objectives first and keep your playing of the scene real and honest. If you played the majority of lines for the subtextual value, there would be no clear, honest relationship developed between the characters.

Literal Sincere-Feeling Lines

This does lead me to talk about something I call "literal sincere-feeling lines." Every audition scene will have dialogue that has sincere-feeling words in it. My direction for those lines is for you to play them for the literal meaning. Most actors just tend to throw these lines away and make them insignificant. Sometimes the actor is not making this mistake by choice, but rather out of ignorance. The following beat will give some obvious examples to work with. A Guy and a Girl who recently broke up and haven't seen each other in a while run into each other at a coffee bar.

                    GUY

When did you get into the city?

                    GIRL

Just yesterday.

                    GUY

You could have called me.

                    GIRL

I'm sorry, I probably should have.

                    GUY

It's all right...I guess. I mean, of course

it's all right. How was the country?

                    GIRL

I loved it. I really had fun.

                    GUY

Great. I have to get going. Let's get

together if you want.

                    GIRL

I'll call you. I promise this time.

                    GUY

Thanks.

I know what you're thinking—boring scene—but let me make my points. There are two very clear literal-feeling lines in this scene. The first is when the Guy tells the Girl that she should have called him to inform him that she was back in town. Her response is, "I'm sorry, I probably should have." That line should be interpreted as a literal sincere-feeling line. In the playing of that line, you simply play it for its literal meaning. The character says she is sorry, so the actress should play it in an apologetic manner. The other literal-feeling line is when the

Girl says, "I loved it. I really had fun," in response to the Guy asking her how she liked her vacation in the country. Once again, the actress should play that line expressing the feeling of love and showing the fun she had on her country trip.

This may seem very simple, but I must stress that in the real world of casting and in my class situations, I find that most actors throw away those lines; they play them as if they are insignificant. That is because the actors are attempting to play a deeper level of subtextual feelings about their relationship with the other person. But the deeper, subtextual feelings the actors are trying to put into their readings are not necessarily what those lines are about. For a first audition, it is much better to have a clear major objective and to play the lines for their literal meaning. Don't stress the subtext; instead, play the moment.

These are free points in an audition. Look at it this way. When actors walk into an audition situation, every one of them is walking on a neutral line. There is no preconceived notion about the actor or her acting ability for the role. The evaluation of the actor and her work comes strictly from the audition. It is in that audition that actors receive symbolic positive points for doing certain things well and negative points for not successfully completing other moments.

So, when you get your sides, you should look for the literal sincere-feeling lines and light up with joy when you see them, because you are basically identifying the places where you can get free, positive points for your audition.

There is not an actor in the world who does not know what it is to love something or someone, to have fun, or to be apologetic for something that has either happened or that she caused in her real life. Those are the feeling words needed for the literal sincere-feeling lines.

You can argue that it is not interesting to play just what is literally meant for the lines. But I am telling you that most auditioning actors do not do the little things well, so if you can do the little things well *and* be supported by a solid technique, you will be in better shape than the actor who plays subtext only and loads every line of dialogue with meanings that are not meant to be there. When you get the callback, you can then flavor those lines with a hint of that subtext—but never let it become the basis for the audition.

CHAPTER 20

The Right Approach, the Right Attitude

If you learn nothing from this book or this technique, please at least learn to have fun when auditioning. If an actor has fun in an audition, then a casting director will have fun. I spoke earlier about how that will help you to be remembered, and it's true. You want to make sure that you incorporate fun into the character. See if there is a moment in the scene to bring a little levity to the situation. You can't force this, but you can look for it. Certainly a very dramatic and emotional scene would not lend itself to having fun, but many scenes do.

Three Minutes of Joy

The best way to bring fun moments to the scene is to have fun yourself. Yes, I mean *you*. I have already depressed you by telling you how many actors are auditioning for the role, and stressed that you are probably not going to get the role. However, if you at least have fun and enjoy the actual audition, the opportunity to act for three minutes should bring you joy. Do not let the frustration and the monotony of the process bring you down. Do not let the stress of life and the real world have a negative effect on your auditions.

I mentioned in chapter 8, "On the Clock", that I am aware that life gets in the way, but you shouldn't let it get in the way of your actual in-the-room audition. I would much rather have actors cancel or reschedule an audition than bring that stress to me. I am a sympathetic person, but I do not have time for any negative influences in an audition. You should also certainly not tell anyone in an audition your problems. Once again, if you have fun, I have fun.

Be Confident

In addition to a sense of fun, you should always bring confidence into your auditions. You should not be confident that you are going to book the role—because we know what the odds of that are—but you should be confident in the choices you have made. You should be confident in the fact that you are well prepared for the audition, and that the audition itself will be a rewarding experience. I don't advise you to be confident that you are going to book the job, because, given the odds, I think that is too much of an emotional roller coaster to put yourself through. Be confident in the homework, be confident in your own skill level, and be confident in the fact that auditioning is the reality of your career, and that, one day, everything will line up for you and you will progress in the process by starting to receive callbacks and bookings.

If you are confident in your choices, that will be evident. Casting directors have confidence in actors who are confident. If actors do not present themselves in a confident manner, then how can a casting director have faith that the actors will succeed in the casting process? I am not telling you to be arrogant. I am saying that you should believe in yourself, and soon others will believe in you too.

CHAPTER 21

Beginnings and Endings

It is vital that you as an actor respect the first and last lines of your sides. Simply put, the first line offers the first impression a casting director will have of you as an actor (not as a person), and the last line is the final impression a casting director will have of you for that audition and role.

Opening Line

The opening line of an audition is very important, and as an actor you should remind yourself of this. In a play, the first time a character is seen is very important for the audience. In a play, the character's first entrance is vital to the audience for getting a sense of who the character is, whether he enters with dialogue or in silence.

In an audition, the first line is your entrance. Your first line of an audition is just as good as an entrance in a play.

Now that you know that the first line is important, what does this mean to you? Well, you have to recognize that your first line is your entrance, and that you are playing to an audience of one—and that is the casting director. So, you must say your line in a way that will get the casting director's attention. I like to describe this by saying that the first line should "pop." It is the first time we hear you speak as character, and you need to make sure that your diction is clear and that you have a purpose to your opening line that both expresses its literal, sincere meaning and displays a clear understanding of your major objective. For example, in the first scene in this book, the Man's first line is, "Are you hungry?" Well, if the Man's major objective is to have a romantic evening with his wife (so that he does not get caught tonight), then his opening line should pop with an energetic tone that communicates that the man is trying to convince his wife it would be fun to go out. However, most actors would just throw that line away, thinking that it is insignificant to the playing of the scene. It's certainly not the most interesting acting moment of the scene, but it launches the audition in the right direction and gets the casting director's attention.

So, be clear with the opening line. Make it pop, have clear diction and pronunciation, and combine it with an understanding of the major objective. Don't overthink or overact this line; after all, it is just a line, and should always be played within the reality of the scene and the environment where it takes place.

Tag Line

The tag line is your last line of the audition. You always want the audition to end with *your* line being the last line, rather than the reader's. There is nothing you can do if you don't have the last line, but I point it out just so that you can recognize your good fortune if you are lucky enough to have audition sides in which you get to have the last word.

If your opening line is equivalent to an entrance in a play, then your tag line is equivalent to your exit line. You want to say the line with a tone that will have the audience (casting director) wanting more. If you watch daytime television, the last line of every scene is an excellent example of how to land a tag line. The exit line should leave the audience with a sense of suspense.

You can also relate the tag line to your major objective. Ask yourself if your character has achieved your major objective or not, and then flavor your tag line with the feeling associated with that achievement or with that lack of success.

In the first scene, the Woman has achieved her objective because she confronted her husband about the affair. Her last line to the Man is, "It actually feels good to finally confront you about it, because I cannot live this lie anymore." If you are the actress doing this audition, you must ask yourself, "How does the character feel about confronting the Man and achieving her major objective?" I would suggest that she feels great about the fact that she confronted him, and, if that is the case, she can land her last line with a sense of accomplishment. She has relieved the pain that she was in. As an actor, you should have an understanding of that in the moment. What happens to her life and her marriage is not your concern in the audition, but it would be nice to button the scene with a sense that there is more to discover.

By the same token, if the Woman did not achieve her major objective, then the delivery of her last line would be reflective of her feeling of not having accomplished her agenda and the pain that she is still in. Either way, there is more to come.

CHAPTER 22

High Stakes and Urgency

I love this point of the technique. I love it because I think it is so vital to every audition, and it is certainly evident in the daytime television audition. Earlier, I mentioned that you probably had some teacher or director mention to you that you need to break a scene down into beats, but he or she probably never clearly explained how to do that. Well, I feel the same way about high stakes and urgency. Chances are, you have been in a scene study class or theatrical production where the director told you and your partner that you needed to raise the stakes in the scene. You nodded your head in acknowledgement of this note, but were unclear on how and why you should be doing that. I will try to explain it for the purposes of the audition.

The Audition Scene Is Important

What "high stakes and urgency" means to me is that you must recognize that the audition scene is the most important moment in your character's life, and you must recognize that the moment is happening right now. (When I say "moment," I mean the scene.) Three pages, five pages, ten pages, it doesn't matter; this event is the most important event that your character is going through. If you recognize the importance of it, it will help you have a better understanding of the level of passion and urgency needed to complete the event. This will assist you in pursuing the major objective and help you dictate the pace of the scene. The urgency is your character's desire to try to achieve his or her major objective *now*—not tomorrow, not yesterday, and not even after the commercial break. The past is behind you, and you know you missed that chance. The future is in front of you, and you do not know what will come of it. The present is the now, so you accept that this is very important (high stakes), and you go after it with passion and desire (urgency) and the need to achieve your objective as soon as possible.

In the first scene, the Woman must recognize that today is the day she will either fix her marriage or walk away from it, and she recognizes that this scene is when she will do that. If she takes a blasé attitude toward her situation, she will not be interesting, because she has not taken an interest in or invested in her circumstances and environment.

If, as an actor in an audition, you play the scene as if it is any old day in your character's life, it will lack stakes and urgency. That is when the note "raise the stakes" is usually introduced. An audition cannot be another day in the life of your character; it has to be the *most important* day in the life of your character. When you recognize that your character has something to gain and also something to lose, it raises the stakes for you. This should not offend the naturalistic actor's sensibility, which leads him to be natural and simple. I implore you to be simple; I just want you to recognize that out of five hundred actors auditioning for this role, the people who are too simple, too run-of-the-mill, get lost in the shuffle of the crowd. Meanwhile, the actor who recognizes that the character has something very important to try to achieve, and then goes about trying to achieve it with urgency, has a better opportunity to be remembered. This will make your audition very active, very present, and very thinking, feeling, and breathing. You will be remembered for being passionate and determined.

CHAPTER 23

Spontaneity and Listening

After the application of an audition technique, after all the work during the On the Clock phase of preparation, after all the memorization, and after the choices you have embodied, you still need your audition to be fresh. This is difficult. If you have worked on a play, you will know that it is almost inevitable that, at some point during the rehearsal process, the company hits a wall; everyone's choices seem stale, and the energy of the work seems to be dulled. This is natural, and easily forgiven in a production process, because there is time to review your choices, both individually and as an ensemble, and to make changes or perhaps just work through the challenges you now face. Many actors carry around a monologue in their memory bank, and even that can be refreshed by a new approach, choice, or piece of blocking (blocking is acceptable for a theatrical monologue). However, when the clock is running on your television audition preparation and you do not have enough time to work through those challenges, you must recognize that you need to remember to be spontaneous and listen.

This is a great challenge, given all the limitations that occur in a television audition. However, it is not impossible. You simply must remind yourself that you are hearing the other character's dialogue for the first time and saying your lines for the first time. Even though you as an actor will have a plan for the business of the audition and your technique has prepared you with your major objective, major beat change, et cetera, you must realize that in order to be fresh, you must be flexible and keep spontaneity in your line readings.

You must be careful not to anticipate the reader's lines because you are so prepared. Anticipation will be evident when you jump on the ends of the reader's lines. When an actor does that, he is accused of not listening, and listening is key to acting. In the audition, you just must recognize that even though you know what you are going to say, you are saying it for the first time. This is difficult; it is where the actor, who is prepared with a plan for the audition, confronts the inherent limitations of that very same plan.

You must trust that your technique and your plan have put you in a very solid position to audition successfully to show your potential. However, you must also be flexible. Let things happen in the audition because of the spontaneous reactions you receive from the reader, the people in the room, and the physical space. This should not cause you to throw away the prepared choices you worked so hard at. The fact that you have gotten to the point where you can listen and respond spontaneously while still using your On the Clock homework should give you every confidence in your choices. They will be there for you if you need to rely on them, but you will still be available to hearing and speaking for the first time. The easiest preparation for this is just to remind yourself when you are in the waiting room that you are saying the lines for the first time and hearing the lines for the first time, and to remember to be available to the reader and his lines.

If you are successful in the early auditions, you will have to work to keep the scene new and fresh, because the further you go in the process, the longer you will have been working on the same material. You must continue to recognize this as you continue and get closer to booking the role. When you get to the screen test, it should still be believable that you are hearing this most important moment for the first time.

CHAPTER 24

Voice and Speech

It is vital to the audition that the actor is comfortable with his own voice and the volume at which he speaks during the audition. Nerves can be an enemy to the actor and to the control of volume. I find that a nervous actor usually speaks too low to be heard, and an anxious actor usually speaks too loudly for the space that the actual audition is being held in. Additionally, all actors must have good diction. It is imperative that every word is clear and audible.

Natural and Conversational Tone

In an audition, you should always be speaking in a natural and conversational tone. You never want to project your voice in a television audition, or speak at a volume that is not natural to the space that you are in. Many theatre actors who are not used to the television audition will have a hard time making this adjustment, because they are used to performing on a stage where projection is required. Singers will have the same challenge, as sometimes their voices are naturally much louder and stronger. Always remind yourself to talk in the manner in which you usually speak. Certainly, acting choices may influence the pitch and emphasis of certain emotional moments in a scene, but by and large, always keep a conversational and natural tone. Actors who do not speak in such a manner run the risk of being labeled "theatrical."

Spatial Relationship

In an audition, your volume should only be loud enough to be heard by the reader and by anyone else who is in the room observing you. You should judge your volume and projection by realizing the relationship you and the reader have as it relates to space. I call this the "spatial relationship." This is very simple. If you are two feet away from the reader, then you speak in a volume that is loud enough to be heard by someone two feet away—no more and no less. If the reader is seven feet away from you, adjust your volume enough to be heard from seven feet and project only enough to cover the distance of the spatial relationship with the reader.

Don't Project

You never want to project above the reader's head and ignore the distance that you are from the reader. So, if the reader is two feet away from you and you are projecting to someone who is seven feet away, then you are really projecting the dialogue of the scene over and beyond what is required in that space. This is when an actor will be accused of being theatrical, since the casting director will envision him on a stage because he is not making any adjustments to the person in front of him in the room.

No Word Is More Important than Any Other Word

Also, when you are speaking in a conversational and natural tone, you want to make sure that you do not stress any words. What I mean by this is that in any sentence of dialogue, you must give equal emphasis to all the words of a sentence, and not indicate that any one word is the most important. Your acting and feeling choices should imbue what you are saying with your feelings, rather than you as an actor forcing that. For example, a line of dialogue, such as, "I love you," should just be said without any emphasis of a single word. It should have emotional empha-sis, but that is not what I am objecting to here. Actors will often try to emphasize a word to make it more significant. An actor can mistakenly choose to put emphasis on the word "love" in the sentence, such as, "I LOVE you." By doing this, the actor will only make the choice stand out as odd, and he will not be effective. You must recognize that "love" is no more important that the words "I" and "you" in that line. There is no reason for the actor to place emphasis on the word by manipulating it vocally. The word "love" is more significant because of the feeling and purpose that is associated with the word, and as an actor, you must concentrate on that.

One handy reminder is to use the punctuation as your guide. Always let the tempo and flow of your speech be guided by the position of the punc-tuation marks. Always let the periods or question marks pull you toward the end of a line. Use the commas to guide you through the sentence to the final punctuation. This will remind you to not hit any words along the way.

CHAPTER 25

Charm, Personality, and Passion

I mentioned earlier that at the basic level in auditioning, regardless of technique and acting ability, casting directors are looking for charming, personable, and passionate people. I would simply like to add that this too is part of your technique. When you enter an audition, I stress that you should have a plan. Part of your plan is to display the choices you made in your preparation time. In addition to that, you must remind yourself of your own level of charm and passion. Everyone has a personality. Many of you use it well, and others let theirs disappear at the onset of nerves and pressure. Do not let this happen, at any cost. The ability to let yourself be yourself will open you up to a world of acting and auditioning responsibilities; sometimes it is just a matter of acknowledging that you have a sense of charm and a level of personality that can assist you.

Don't Fake It

Also, please do not ever try to fake charm. A young actor came to see me one day to audition for a new contract role. When I say "young," I mean he was in his early twenties and a bit new to the process. When I greeted him in the waiting room, he gave me a very big and firm handshake, one that I would describe as larger than normal. I remember trying not to think too much about it. When we got to my office, he made several comments about how nice my office was, asking about photographs that I had of my family on my desk. This bothered me because I felt like asking about my personal things and about people close to me may have been crossing some sort of professional line. I realize I have those on my desk and may be inviting a reaction, but he seemed to go overboard. However, he was young, so I gave him the benefit of the doubt, hoping he would relax.

He didn't. When I tried to find out a little about him to better understand him, he answered every question by addressing me with a new nickname, like "Buddy," "Pal," or "Dude." At this point, I was less than thrilled, and he had not even read yet. I was angry and frustrated and passing judgment before he even read, but he had created this atmosphere—I didn't. When we finally got to reading, I was looking forward to his act of charm leaving, but it only continued. He insisted on ad-libbing these nicknames during the course of the scene. After every few lines, he would address me (or the character) by "Dude" and "Bud." This really distracted me from the reading, and when the scene was done, I told him so. I was so frustrated by this that I actually felt the need to educate him about the process and about what is considered acceptable and what isn't.

His response was simple: He said he was a charming guy who was a little nervous, and when he gets nervous, he tries to relax the people around him by making them feel comfortable. Ironically, I was comfortable before he started this nonsense, and I told him so. Unfortunately, I will probably never give this actor another opportunity to audition for me. The lesson is to be yourself and allow your personality to come out, but don't let it overwhelm you and be what you are about.

Passion

A note on passion: You must be aware of your level of passion, both as a character and as an actor. As an actor, you must find the strength to persevere in your career; as a character, you must find the strength to pursue your major objective. Passion is a very appealing characteristic for actors to have. That passion comes from the work, and you must bring it to the work. In your career, you will audition more than you will act, so be passionate about the process. Be excited for the opportunity, and then find the passion in your choices and in your character.

CHAPTER 26

The Acting Part

Innate talent cannot be taught. Many actors have natural instincts that assist them in the choices they make. Others need a lot of hard work with an endless amount of coaching and classes to keep their craft fresh. While this book lays out a very specific audition technique, you as an actor will have to bring your unique choices to the work to make it come to life. An actor's individual understanding of his own craft and his unique imagination allows him to make choices that are special to him. This is another reason why two actors auditioning for the same role, with the same audition sides, will have two completely different auditions. It is those individual choices and each individual's unique body of knowledge that will balance out the audition technique in this book.

You learn your craft in school, by studying with the best teachers and by working in the theatre—being in great plays and hopefully playing great roles. You have an acting technique and a process that works for you, and you continue to develop it while being involved in many projects. The emotional truth that every actor must find in his individual work, whether in a play, an audition, a monologue, a small role in a film or a television show, is vital to his success. His individual perception will guide and advance him. On a very small level, the audition is an actor's opportunity to display those interpretations. The technique is just a format to give you structure to use the words to create a living, thinking, feeling being.

You can decide what your feeling and subject words per beat are, but if you cannot *embody* the feelings about the subject in relation to the other person in the scene, then you are only doing scene analysis without the physical and emotional requirements needed. Acting is an athletic endeavor, like any regular sport. Just like basketball or bowling, it requires physical engagement, along with strong willpower and focus. Technique is the architectural plans to build a house, but if you don't pick up a hammer to build the house, you are just an architect. As an actor, you must be the architect *and* the builder, bringing physical and athletic life to the plans that you have created.

Don't Forget to Breathe!

Many young actors make the mistake of forgetting to do something in their auditions that we do every minute of every day: breathe. Many actors forget to breathe. They don't pass out from this, but many simply do not regulate their breathing properly for an audition. This is directly related to nerves and vulnerability. Oxygen carries emotions in it. If you ever watch anyone who is very emotional, weeping and sobbing, she does not really crescendo her emotions until she starts to take deep breaths, which only causes her to get more emotional. The reason she needs to take deep breaths in the first place is because she is holding her breath in and fighting the emotions she has. When the body allows itself to be vulnerable, it will allow itself to breathe and, in a sense, accept the emotions associated with that oxygen. The same is true for someone who is really angry. He is usually holding his breath in as he is holding his anger in, trying to stay in control of his emotions. When he breathes in, the anger gets released. How does understanding this help you when you are auditioning?

You must recognize that when you are nervous about your audition, you are really nervous because you feel vulnerable. To control that vulnerability, your body shuts off its breathing, and only allows breath in as needed. It is imperative when you are sitting in the waiting room that you make sure that you are breathing normally. If you can get yourself to breathe regularly, you will now be more emotionally available to the feelings of the scene. For example, you will be vulnerable to your character's pain. Remember, if your character is in pain, the major objective you choose should be to relieve that pain. The more available you are to the character's vulnerability, the greater level of success you may have.

How to Remind Yourself

There are two pieces of advice that I have for dealing with breathing. One is to arrive at your audition at least twenty minutes before you're scheduled to actually audition. If you arrive early, you can sit, relax, refresh yourself on your choices, and take the time to acknowledge where your breathing is. Life is hard enough, and it makes us put up natural defense mechanisms to close off the outside world. Actors rushing around New York City are rushing around not breathing because if they breathe in too much, they are vulnerable to the outside. The body's instinct is to protect itself by shutting down. In fact, *no one* wants to walk around Manhattan making eye contact with strangers and feeling vulnerable, so what happens is that there are legions of people (actors and non-actors) walking around New York not breathing properly. Next time you are on a subway, check out all the people staring at the floor or the ceiling, trying to not invite anyone or anything into their space.

This is good in the real world, but not for auditioning, especially when you are late for auditions. I often come out into a waiting room full of non-breathing actors. The more experienced actors always seem more relaxed, but young people new to the process seem to be tense. In addition to any audition nerves they have, they are still closing themselves off from the realities of the outside world. So, get there early and shake off the world. A great relaxation exercise is to sit in the waiting room quietly and just regulate your breathing by inhaling through your nose until your diaphragm and lungs fill up, and then out through your mouth. Inhale through your nose, and then exhale out through your mouth. Repeat this exercise until you are calm.

Use Your Feeling Word

Now, the second piece of advice is directly related to this exercise, and it gets back to the use of your invaluable sides. If you have done the breathing exercise, you can now incorporate it into the opening line of your audition. Before you begin the audition, you look at your feeling word for the opening beat and simply try to feel that feeling as you breathe in through your nose, accept that oxygen and the emotional feeling associated with the word. And then, when you are ready, exhale out your mouth while speaking your first and very important opening line. In chapter 21 I discussed how important the opening line is. This method will make sure that you give the opening line its true importance and that you have jump-started your audition by simply breathing in the feeling (and taking in air). When actors have trouble breathing in an audition, it is usually evident in the opening beat, and their body never catches up. My hope here is that you can kick-start your instrument.

Only those actors who are nervous and recognize their own breathing limitations should be using this exercise. I strongly urge you to practice this when you are On the Clock, so that you are not surprised by the results in the room. Perhaps the more you practice this, the less you need it. The bottom line is that you have to find a way to relax for the audition, and arriving early is good standard advice anyway.

CHAPTER 28

The On-Camera Audition

Many times, a casting director will have the need to videotape your audition. In my daytime television work, I usually do not do this, but I have had to on occasion if the executive producer's schedule and the actor's schedule do not coincide. However, I have done this many times for Los Angeles–based projects I may be working on in New York. I also mentioned that in my search for a contract actor, I videotape all my Los Angeles–based callbacks to show to the executive producer.

Usually, an actor will be put on tape for the callback stage of auditioning, rather than the first audition. Many casting directors and productions work in different ways, but my experience has been that videotaping is mostly for a callback. If you take my advice from this technique and remove all forms of staging from your audition, you will be in an excellent place to make an adjustment to the on-camera audition. My advice has been to simply sit or stand for your entire audition. If the casting director instructs you that he wants to put you on tape, you really do not have to make any major adjustments to your reading, because movement is the biggest element that gets in the way of an on-camera audition. If time is running out and the need to cast a role is becoming urgent, many times a casting director will have a first audition with an actor, then decide to put him on camera right at that very moment. If you have been moving around during your first audition and are now told to stand still for the camera, you will probably feel very physically uncomfortable making that adjustment. Even if you were told to come back another day you would have time to remove any staging before the callback taping, but now you are doing extra work that is unnecessary. If you were sitting in the first audition, you can now just sit for your callback.

Something to remember about on-camera auditions is that many times the casting director is operating the camera as well as reading with you. He would not have the ability to move the camera while you walk in the space and simultaneously say lines.

Do I Look at the Camera?

If you are being put on tape, always speak directly to the reader, not the camera, unless instructed to do so. If you are unfortunate enough to have a scene with two other characters in it, you can create the illusion that there are two people in the room off camera by speaking directly to the reader (usually just off camera on one side) and placing the other imaginary character off camera to the opposite side.

You Have to Pop off the Screen

One trick to doing an on-camera audition is to remember to drive the audition scene. For some reason, and some people disagree with me on this, I find that an actor reading on tape actually plays back slower than it seemed to play in real time in the room. Technology actually gets in the way of pacing. You always want to pop off the screen for those who are watching you, so driving the scene is a suitable way to fight the technical playback. This could be my perception of things, but it still can't hurt to keep your energy up.

Slating

You will always be required to slate on camera before your reading. This moment usually requires the actor to state his name directly to the camera. Many times, you will also be asked to give the name of your agent/manager, your height, or the name of the role you are reading for. Just make sure that you are paying attention when the casting director tells you what information she would like in the slate. You do not want to have to re-slate because you did not provide the required information.

Always make sure that you know whether the camera will be shut off after you slate or if the camera will continue to roll, leading into the scene. This is important because you have to be prepared for either type of taping, and you want to look professional. When you slate, you should always stand up straight, smile, and show that personality I have been talking about. Assume that someone important will see this, and your slate is his first impression of you. You want him to *want* to see you act. After giving the necessary information, hold your natural smile until the camera is paused. If the camera will continue rolling, take a second after the slate (and smile) to prepare for the audition. Make a clear transition from you the actor to you the character. This does not require a long silent pause of preparation, but rather a moment of transition to remind yourself of your major objective.

What to Wear

If you can, try to find out what color background you will be standing in front of when being put on tape. You never want to wear the same color as the background, or you run the risk of blending into it. So, if the backdrop is black, don't wear black clothes (a tough feat in New York), and if it is blue, don't wear blue. As you go along in your career and meet with casting directors, you should make every effort to remember what color background they use for the tapings.

CHAPTER 29

The Cold Reading Audition

Cold reading auditions are when you have very little time to prepare for the audition—usually around five minutes. I don't like to do this to an actor, but sometimes you have a meeting with someone, and then you get an idea that he might be right for a role, so you hand him some sides and ask him to look at them. Many actors will choose to read the scene several times and just wing it in the room. However, I feel that a shorter version of the technique can be applied to have a successful audition. This would be your five-minute On the Clock preparation.

How to Break It Down

If you find yourself in this situation, get a pencil, read the scene, and then concentrate solely on beats, the major beat change, and the major objective. You will, of course, quickly make decisions about the backstory and the relationship in the scene. By doing the beats, you will give yourself the beat change marks to drive the scene and give yourself structure. By determining the major objective, you will have made a decision as to what your character wants from the scene, and by marking the major beat change, you will have decided what the most important moment of the scene is for your character—and if he achieves his major objective or not. These simple steps will give you focus and direction while under the pressure of limited time. If you have additional time, you can move on to the subject and feeling words, but I don't think this is as important when you are pressed for time. Once you have made your choices and written on your sides, spend the remaining time getting familiar with the dialogue. Do not make an effort to memorize the sides; it is a waste of time and not the attribute that will get you another audition or the job.

CHAPTER 30

Under-5 and Background Work in Daytime Television

There is a slight controversy and conflicting opinions about this among my daytime casting director peers as well as among producers and directors. However, this is my book, so I am going to give you my honest opinion on the subject of actors doing under-5 and background work in daytime television.

Take the Work and Get the Experience

Without any doubt or hesitation, I recommend that any young actor who wants to break into television *should* do background and under-5 work on a daytime television show. Let me explain. There are four daytime shows in New York, and five in Los Angeles. The sets on a daytime television program are intimate and small. If you are a smart actor, you will take advantage of the opportunity to learn on the set while doing background work. You may be a patron in our restaurant scene, and sitting at the booth across from you are two actors with thirty years of experience between them. Don't you think you can learn something from watching them? Also, I would watch how the stage manager interacts with the actors, how the director interacts with both the actors and the stage manager, and so on. Perhaps you will even get lucky and be given some direction, like being told to make an exit or cross to another patron's table. Because the sets are so small, you have a good chance of being seen on camera, which is of course exciting for a young actor. You get paid for the day, and, if you want, you can put it on your resume, too. It is a legitimate credit and a wonderful experience.

Let me be clear. I am talking about daytime television, where there is the intimacy of the set and where the hours are shorter than on films or primetime productions. I am not talking about filling a seat at Yankee Stadium for a movie. Although one should experience such an event at least one time in his or her career, I don't think it is as rewarding and educational as the daytime experience.

You Never Know What Can Happen

I am also a strong believer that you have to be involved to make things happen. You never know what other actors you meet in the dressing rooms are doing in their own careers. Perhaps some actor is starting a theatre company and asks you to be a part of it. Another tells you about an open call for a student film, and perhaps another is directing a play reading and wants you involved. The point is, those things can't happen if you are not there. It is very simple to me: Would you rather be on a television set today, or be home watching television? If you are serious about this, there is only one answer. Would you rather be at the restaurant working, or be on a television set? It is clear to me: You take the work and the experience.

Under-5 Work

I have the same feeling toward doing under-5 roles. You should only be so lucky to have five lines on a television show. You get paid, you get the experience, and you start building a career. I am not saying that this is a career, but it is the start of a career. Many actors think there is some stigma attached to doing an under-5, and I think this is strictly because it has the term "under-5" connected to it. There isn't a young actor out there who would turn down a line or two on *Law & Order*; why would you turn down the same opportunity in daytime? Many of our under-5 actors work in a recurring capacity on the show. Actors who play policemen and nurses have been known to work ten to twenty or so episodes a year. Not a career, but part of a career. Take the work when you can get it.

You Are Protecting a Career
You Do Not Have Yet

Now, I know what you are thinking, because I have heard it a hundred times before. You are saying to yourself that if you do background and under-5 work, you will not be considered for bigger parts. My answer to that line of thinking is that you are protecting a career you do not have yet. Don't worry about the what-ifs; deal with the now. The truth of the matter is that you are not being considered for those roles because you are not ready for those roles. I have also stressed to you in the book that you are not going to book that role anyway, if you are lucky enough to even get an audition for it. We have twenty to thirty under-5 and background roles a week. There may be three to five day players a month and two to three significant roles a year, and most actors want to wait for them when they have little to no experience as it is. The chance that you will be the right type for the role and be good enough for the role and audition well for the role is a long shot.

To reassure you that you will not be limited if you do this work, let me bring a little logic to bear on the conversation. If I am casting a major role and you get an audition for it and you are perfect for it, do you think I will not hire you because you were eating a hamburger in the restaurant in a previous episode? I would be a really bad casting director if I let that stand in the way. Think about it for second. If you were perfect, I wouldn't care what you played before; you would be eligible for the role.

I have an actor on the show right now who has been recurring for a few years. I didn't know this actor before I met him. In his audition, he was good; he showed a lot of potential. When I asked him what he was doing that Wednesday—because I wanted him to have a callback—he informed me that he was working. I asked him if he could get out of work, and he asked me the same thing, because he was working as an extra for the show. Now, when he told me that, my perception of him didn't change. I didn't take back the callback because I thought he was a limited actor; rather, I was glad to see he was working. My associate replaced him for the episode he was supposed to be in, and he went to the callback and booked the job.

Don't wait for an opportunity that may never come. You must create opportunities, and opportunities come from experience and from meeting people. I am not saying that this is a career. You must determine how many times you are willing to do background work. Hopefully, if you do it several times and make a good impression, then you will be asked to read for an under-5 role. There is no promise of that, but you have a better chance of that happening if you have been developing you relationship with the casting office.

Additionally, whenever I have a contract role, I ask my staff to make a list of actors whom they have hired and whom I do not know who may be right for the role I am casting. Most of these actors do not have agents, but I will give those actors an opportunity to read for the contract. This is my staff, whom I trust. Why wouldn't I read another five actors when I am already reading three to five hundred? Now, there is no guarantee of that happening, but the point is that you will be creating a relationship with a casting office and making some effort to progress in your career. It certainly cannot happen if you are not there.

Other people will tell you that you should not do the smaller roles because you need to hold out for bigger ones. It is worth repeating: You are protecting a career that you do not have yet. Don't protect the future. If you are the best person for a role, nothing should stand in the way of you obtaining it. Nothing in your career is achieved by sitting on your couch and daydreaming about it.

CHAPTER 31

The Under-5 Audition

Hopefully, I have convinced you to do under-5 and background work. Now, I want to briefly discuss the under-5 audition. There is no audition for doing background work. Usually that involves a meeting with an associate casting director so that she can get a sense of the actor's personality and level of responsibility.

Technique

An audition for an under-5 role may be one of the hardest auditions in television. You would think that because it is short—fewer than five lines—it would be easier than a contract audition, but this is not necessarily the case. This lesson on under-5 auditions can also be applied to any television audition for what would be considered a small role. The key to the under-5 audition is to recognize that the audition scene is not about you. I know that may be hard to grasp when it is your audition, but unlike the contract role, this audition is strictly about proving that you can blend into the fabric of the production. When you realize and accept that the scene is not about you—that you are just a moment in a leading character's life—you can approach the audition with those fundamentals in mind. Think about your real life, and how many people pass in and out of it everyday. The man at the deli, the woman standing in line in front of you at Starbucks, the taxi driver, or the man in the elevator who has asked you to press his floor. All of those people are under-5 actors in the television show that is your life. They come and go, and that is exactly what you need to display in the audition for the role.

You forget about beats and major beat changes. You need only decide what your major objective is and what your subject and feeling words are. There will only be one beat, so there are no beat changes, and only one subject word and one feeling word for you to concentrate on. You decide what your character wants, and you do it, getting in and out of the other character's life.

In the actual room audition, you can even emphasize this acceptance that it is the other person's scene by walking into the space (not from outside the door, just from the side) to the center of the room, saying your lines, and then exiting to the other side. I am not contradicting my own "no blocking" rule, because this behavior is appropriate for this type of audition. If there is not enough space to do that move, then you should just turn from the side to face the reader, and then turn away at the end. There is something symbolic about showing the casting director that I can walk into the other person's life, be there for a moment, and then be out of his or her life as quickly as I came into it. For those of you who question my thinking that the scene is not about you, you should remind yourself that if you book the job, you will get paid about $350 for that day of work, and that the other person is getting a few thousand a week. Who do you think the camera is really going to be focused on?

Below, please find an example of what an under-5 audition may look like. Look at this from the nurse's point of view.

```
Hospital. Morning. A doctor is looking through some
files at the nurse's station.

He sips a cup of coffee. The nurse enters.


                    NURSE

        Doctor, I have the x-rays you requested.

                    DOCTOR

        How does it look?

                    NURSE

        Not that promising.
```

```
                    DOCTOR

        Would you please inform the patient that we

        have the results back?

                    NURSE

        I am on my way now.

She exits.
```

If you are auditioning for the nurse and you try to make more of this scene than it is, you will come across as overacting. If you consider this scene to be insignificant, then you will just be standing there and saying your lines in a very lackadaisical fashion. But, if you recognize that you are a moment in the doctor's life, you will come into the scene with energy, pass along the information that is required, and then move off to get to the next piece of business that is required of your character.

From a technique perspective, you have one beat, which is the entire scene. You have no beat changes, and your major objective is to inform the doctor about the x-rays and results in a professional manner. You should do that with a sense of energy, to display your understanding that you are a small part of the doctor's life at that moment. If you book the job, and the director wants you to do something else, then you can make that adjustment on the set. Even in auditioning for the small role, the way in which you *audition* for the role and the way you *perform* the role may be different.

Perhaps, if you book the job, the director of the show will want to make something of the scene, and will suggest that you flirt with the doctor. In that case, do what the director says. However, if you try flirting in the audition, the associate casting director will be fearful that you will make too much of the few lines you have and will probably not hire you.

CHAPTER 32

I Wouldn't Do That If I Were You

What you should do and what you shouldn't do in a casting director's office seems like it would be obvious, but, unfortunately, many actors need guidance on this. This will be an honest sharing of information that I think will be helpful to every young actor. Many of these things have happened to me, and they are easily fixed if the actor is aware of the negative things he is doing.

Do's

Some of the things on the "to do" list are: be prepared, be on time (if not a little early), and be comfortable with your sides, but not memorized. Be gracious about having been given the opportunity to audition and be seen, always have an additional headshot and resume on you at all times, and always look your best. You should have a plan for your audition, including what you will do when you enter the room and also how you will exit the room when the audition is done.

Don'ts

Things that should *never* happen in an audition are: never forget to bring your sides, never bring a negative attitude into the audition, and don't ever feel defeated or express that you are not right for the role. Don't ask the casting director if you can do the scene again, and don't, before the audition starts, tell the casting director that you would be happy to do the audition again at the end if he or she would like. (We will ask if we want you to!) Don't ask the casting director when you are done whether he or she would like you to send the next person in. Don't expect to get feedback for the audition or ask when the callbacks are going to be.

Get in and Get Out

In continuing with the need to pass out advice, I can't think of any better advice than telling an actor to get in and get out of the audition room. I'm basically telling you not to overstay your welcome. This is all part of having a plan before you enter the room. I want to talk about some things that most people probably never talk about, but which they do stew over. When you are auditioning, you should never bring too much extra baggage into the room. Not emotional baggage—although I have already covered the need to leave that at home—but physical baggage. I cannot stand it when actors do not have their sides out and ready. When I want to start an audition, I want to be able to start the audition; I don't want to wait for an actor to open his bag, or briefcase, and find the folder that the sides are in. I just want to start. By the same token, I do not want to wait after the audition is over for the actor to put the sides away in the folder and then back into the bag, to close the bag, and then to leave. This seems like it takes an eternity to do, especially when no one is talking. When the audition is over, I do not want to make small talk about the weather; I want to move on, because I am busy. One of two things happens when the audition is over and I say, "Thanks for coming." An actor will either slowly gather up his belongings in silence, or he will begin to chitchat with me about things I am not interested in.

Both situations are awkward, and I believe both can hurt your evaluation. Perhaps your actual audition puts you in the "maybe" pile; if you do something that turns a casting director off by making him feel uncomfortable, it can have a negative effect on his perception of you. I don't want to seem unreasonable, and I am not suggesting that any actor would lose a job over this or behave this way in order to be intentionally annoying, but that makes it even more frustrating. Be a professional and think about the bigger picture, like how busy a casting director is. Don't come in with the bag in the first place, and if you do, then know enough when the audition is over to just grab your stuff and leave. You can very easily get yourself resituated back in the waiting room.

Don't Forget Your Props and Stuff

If you use props, when the audition is over you will spend a lot of time searching for those props. If you happen to carry your cell phone or your sunglasses into the room, when it is time to go you will need to spend time gathering those belongings up. My point is that they don't belong there anyway. Wintertime in New York is the worst offender in terms of encouraging bad habits, because actors will come in with large winter coats, hats, scarves, and gloves. Not only is it bulky, but all of the layers take time to gather up and put on. None of this should be happening when an audition is over and there is only silence. So, have a plan and know what you are bringing into the room and what you shouldn't be bringing into the room with you. Be prepared and be professional. Leave your coat in the waiting room.

CHAPTER 33

Building a Relationship with the Casting Director

As a professional actor, you must develop relationships with the casting directors who give you your auditions. The relationship with a casting director begins with your first audition and is then measured by the amount of actual return auditions you have for that same casting director. This relationship is strictly a business relationship. It is vital for an actor, no matter what coast he is on, to learn which casting directors are working at which offices on that coast. You must then start to build a professional relationship with them through your auditions and follow-up skills. Once you have had your first audition with a casting director, it is really up to you, the actor, to stay in touch and keep him apprised of your work. The relationship is really based on how successful of an auditioner you are. Casting directors will give most any actor several auditions to evaluate his talent before deciding that this is a person they do not need to see anymore. If your auditioning skills are good, the relationship with the casting director will be good, because the casting director will feel the need to keep watching your skills develop and then keep trying to find a role for you. If, in the interview phase of your first audition, you come across as an intelligent, personable actor whom the casting director deems likeable, you will have a better chance of receiving another audition, and then another, for that same casting director. The number of auditions you have for any new roles at that office will have a direct correlation to the relationship you have with that particular casting director and the amount of progress you are making in your career.

The Follow-Up and Staying in Touch

It is very important for you to stay in touch with a casting director in general, and certainly after an audition. Even if you have an agent or manager, you should still take this upon yourself. The personal touch is always best and seems to stand out. A simple note, thanking the casting director for the opportunity to audition and mailed out a few days after the audition, is appropriate. In the note you should always mention the role you came in for and perhaps even what day it was. A postcard-sized headshot should be included with the note so that the casting director has a visual to better remember you by.

You should always stay in touch with a casting director by making him aware of any upcoming theatre projects or showcases you might be in. You should also let casting directors know of any television productions you have booked and when they might be airing. I always try to catch the other New York television productions, and if I am informed that you will be in a certain episode, I am more likely to be looking for you in it. In terms of theatre productions and showcases, it is sometimes just as important to know that you are busy and working as it is to actually see your production, although we try to attend as often as we can.

Keeping a casting director apprised of your work and progress will help nurture this relationship. This relationship could take years to pay off in terms of actually booking a job, but that is all right. The real purpose of this relationship is to obtain an opportunity from it. Opportunity is evidenced by auditions. Relationships with casting directors are like any other relationships: There are some that are stronger than others, and it is up to the actor to see where his efforts are best placed. There are certain casting directors who are just not fans of certain actors' work (it's not personal), and that may hinder those actors' opportunities to receive more auditions. If an actor realizes that, then perhaps he spends less time trying to develop that relationship. Perhaps he decides that relationship is not worth pursuing anymore. That is just the way it is. By the same token, many actors do not like certain casting directors' styles but still have to audition for them in an effort to try to book a job. Remember, this is a business and a business relationship, and each side should remind itself of that.

How to Begin That Relationship

Unless you have an agent or manager, it is very difficult to begin that relationship with a casting director. There is no doubt about that. I am not going to mislead anyone in this book and say that it is easy to get top television auditions without a good agent or manager in your corner making those initial introductions. However, there is always a way, and, at the very least, you should always make an effort. You should always send mailings to the casting directors, inviting them to see your showcases and telling them about your progress. If the information falls on deaf ears, then so be it. However, you never know what can happen, so you must take this action. My best advice to the actor who does not have an agent is just as you would for an audition, set obtainable goals. Instead of writing to the head of casting at a major network, write to an independent casting director who specializes in small independent films or small regional theatre productions. You have a much better chance of starting a relationship with a person who is working on those kinds of projects, and there is absolutely nothing wrong with that. Also, as mentioned in the section about under-5 and background work in daytime, you should write to the associate casting director who is casting those kinds of roles. Set attainable goals for work, so you can meet reachable people. Those reachable people might be open to a business relationship that can benefit both of you. Also, the casting director at a small office this year may move to a large network job next year. If you have a relationship with him, then you are in his hip pocket when he makes his own career move.

No Tricks, Please

Please do not rely on any tricks to try to jump-start a relationship with a casting director or an agent. I personally have never (and don't know any colleagues who have ever) brought in people who have sent us balloons, candy, or anything else you can imagine, along with their headshots or showcase invitations. Just think about yourself for a second and think about whether that is the first impression you want to put out there. In addition, I don't want actors to spend additional money on these gimmicks. It is expensive enough to do the mass mailings, without all the unnecessary bells and whistles attached. I understand the desire to stand out, but ultimately it is your talent and professionalism that will make you do that, not some scheme to be seen.

CHAPTER 34

The Business of Acting and a Career

In the children's fable "The Tortoise and the Hare", the tortoise slowly makes his way through the race and wins as the hare, who was once bragging, now sleeps. This is an excellent metaphor for a career as an actor. Aim to be slow and steady. Most actors have to slowly build their career—from their high school drama club, college theatre productions, graduate school, endless classes, coaching sessions, Off-Off-Broadway theatre, and infinite showcases to small roles in television and film. During that time, they are picking up lessons on how to survive as an actor as they keep building their craft. What is most important from a business perspective is that you begin to develop and then nurture relationships with casting directors.

Learn the Craft

Every week, busloads of people pull into New York City and Los Angeles and pronounce themselves actors as soon as their feet hit the ground. It is a very simple question: Would you like to be someone who *calls* himself an actor, or would you like to be someone who knows and appreciates what it is like to *work* on the skills of becoming an actor? I implore you to be the latter. What you do with these skills, in an effort to make a living, is where the *business* of acting comes in to play.

Talent Is a Guarantee of Nothing

Unfortunately, in this business, talent is a guarantee of nothing. If you divide all of the people who want to be actors into three groups, you would have the most talented people in one group (this would include actors whose skill comes naturally and have now honed their skill by studying), the middle group would include actors who have average talent and skill and have to work that much harder at it to stay fresh, and the third group would include people who lack talent completely (no matter how hard they try, this is not really their game). Well, this business does not guarantee that everyone in the first group will have a successful career. If anything, a percentage of each group will become successful and have a multi-level career. Many will work all the time, many will make a living at it, and some will even reach that rare level of stardom. This is sad for the talented, hard-working actors left behind without a career. Often, in my "civilian" life, I will look at someone, at the gas station or the grocery store, and wonder if she once had the desire to be an actor and if she just never pursued it or if she tried and never got the opportunity to succeed. Ultimately, as an actor you cannot worry where you fall in these groups, but you can worry about how much of an effort you are making toward succeeding. So, study the craft and learn the business to give yourself the best opportunity to succeed.

The Business

No one teaches the business side of acting; I think this is one of the great misfortunes in the industry and in schools around the country. Yes, the actors coming out of the best programs are better prepared for a career because of their advanced level of understanding of the craft, but most actors learn the business by trial and error and repetition. The actor who auditions the most will have the opportunity to get better at auditioning because of that repetition. Repetition breeds familiarity. For many actors, the business will always remain a mystery.

The Tools of the Business

The tools of the business range from knowing what resources are available to you as an actor to many of the approaches I have discussed in this book. I discussed that mass mailings to agents and casting directors are vital, so you must learn that *Ross Reports* is a monthly publication that lists every agent and casting director's name and address. If you do not have an agent, then you must buy *Backstage* every Thursday (or you can subscribe to the online version at *www.backstage.com*), because that is where you will be given audition information on such projects as student films and theatre showcases, which won't require you to have representation. You need to be reading industry magazines such as *Daily Variety*, the *Hollywood Reporter*, and *Entertainment Weekly* to be current on what is happening in the industry.

The Business Approach

When a businessman starts a new venture, he writes a business plan wherein he maps out what the new venture is, what the assets of the business are, how he would like the business to grow, and what he is going to do to implement the venture's success. When I propose a businesslike approach to an acting career, I suggest that you as an actor need a game plan for how you would like your career to go. You must decide what the attainable goals are for you and then try to attain those goals. Deciding you want to get off the bus and become a television star is an unrealistic goal. You can get off the bus, but it is unlikely someone will award you with a career. However, setting goals such as gaining experience in a particular medium is realistic.

You could begin mapping out a career by making a plan to do background work on a daytime television program, with the hope of building a relationship with the casting department. You might also decide to make every effort to get into an Off-Off-Broadway showcase so that you can invite agents to come see it. After completing those goals, you might decide your next step is student films or regional theatre, or perhaps it is a small speaking part on a primetime television show, with the hope that you will be able to develop a demo tape to send to agents as you seek representation. These goals should be set with the idea of accomplishing them within a certain time frame.

Once you have achieved those goals, you can claim a certain level of success and experience. When you employ the audition technique detailed in this book, you are utilizing a very businesslike approach to the art of auditioning because you are setting attainable goals at every level; you can do the same in your career as a whole. While pursuing your goals, you are studying and learning and working your "money job" to help support this investment in the career that you are making for yourself. This plan does not guarantee success; it only guarantees fulfillment of goals. If you do develop a successful career, even better. I am sure this is better than the young actor sitting in his studio apartment, watching television and waiting for the phone to ring to ask him to be on the television program he is watching. It just does not happen that way.

You must treat your acting career like a business, because the business will treat you that way. It is not unheard of for an actor to go through the entire audition process and land a role, only to have that role be recast during production. This is not personal; it is usually a business decision. You spend good money on your headshots and resumes and mailing them to people, and they end up in the trash. This isn't personal; it is the reality of the business. Network television is a big business that involves a lot of advertising dollars, and sometimes the people who have the ultimate casting decisions have to think about that as well.

CHAPTER 35

Getting an Agent or a Manager

I don't know how this is done. I mean it—I really don't know how you do this. I wish there were a simple explanation, but there is not. How can there be, when some of the most talented people out there do not have representation? Still others have been discovered working at a restaurant or standing on the subway. The following is some advice on how to go about trying to get an agent. It is certainly not a guarantee, but perhaps it's some advice in the right direction.

Go to School

The best opportunity I know of to get an agent or manager is to go to a training program that offers an industry showcase before graduation. Many of the best programs around the country will come to New York or Los Angeles with their graduating class and do a presentation of scenes to the industry, with the hope that their students will obtain meetings with agents, casting directors, and managers. This seems to me to be the best way to start a career and get those desirable meetings. I don't care how old or young you are—I am a big believer in getting training. If the program you choose is a good program, you will get anywhere from two to four years of college- or conservatory-level training. That means learning the craft and working on the best plays, doing the best roles. That industry showcase is a wonderful opportunity to transition from the study of the craft to the business of acting and a career.

Write to the Assistant

My only other advice on obtaining an agent or manager would be to try to make contact with an assistant at an office. This is also practical advice in the pursuit of getting a casting person to see your work in a theatrical production. If you want to get an agent, and you write the head agent at a large talent agency and invite him to come see you in a showcase or request a meeting, chances are that those requests will fall on deaf ears because those people will be too busy to deal with you. That is just the truth. The head of a major agency is not going to have time to read your invitation to a showcase, much less attend it, but his assistant might. Not only do you have a better chance of getting your mail read, but you also have an even better chance of getting an assistant to attend your showcase.

You see, the thinking is that the assistant will not be an assistant for long. If you can create a relationship with that person, then hopefully one day, when that person is promoted or leaves his current company to take a better position in another agency, he will remember you. At some point in every young casting assistant or agent assistant's career, he will be asked to make a contribution to the company. That contribution could be creating a list of actors for a part, reading actors for a role, or attending a showcase and reporting back to the boss on who he liked. He will be given an opportunity to prove himself. What you want to be able to do is create a relationship with that person, so that when he has to step up, you are one of the people he feels confident in. This is a business where the talented people can move up quickly. I went from a casting assistant to an associate to the casting director of the longest-running program in broadcast history all within two and a half years. I know agent assistants at one company who leave to become agents at another within a few years. They will need people to help them make a transition. So, send your mail to the assistant. Believe me, when he is opening hundreds of pieces of mail that are addressed to the person he works for, and then gets a piece of mail addressed to him, it makes him feel special.

Get a Friend to Help You

Lastly, if your friend has an agent, beg the friend to make an introduction for you. But you had better be ready to perform at your best if you are given the opportunity to meet the agent, because you may not get a second chance.

CHAPTER 36

Headshots and Resumes

I cannot think of anything I like to discuss less than actors' headshots and resumes. I have two very simple thoughts regarding what actors should be concerned about when choosing pictures.

Look Like Your Picture

The old saying is true: Make sure you look like your picture. Don't get a very glamorous picture of yourself, if that's not what you look like. All casting directors want to see when you show up to meet them for the first time is that you look like what they expect; what they expect is the person in the photo.

One Shot Only, Please

Second, do not spend additional money getting extra copies of you in several different poses. I personally do not know the difference between a theatrical shot, a commercial shot, a soap shot, a sitcom shot, and a film shot. Actors often will give me a different headshot from the one I have of them, claiming that they have a more appropriate look and picture for daytime. Is this because they were not smiling, as opposed to the shot where they were smiling? Does that mean that if you have a serious look on your face, you are a serious dramatic actor? But if you have a smile, that means you are funny and have a great personality? Is this like saying that when you send me a comp card with pictures of you dressed as a cop or a doctor or a pirate, that is the only thing you can play? Stop the madness. Do you think I wouldn't hire you because you were smiling or not, or standing or not, or making funny faces or not in your picture? To me, it is all about the work, not the photo. I recognize that the photo is important because it is really your first opportunity to be seen, but you just need to have one very good one that looks like you. If it can show some personality, great, but I am a not sure that can be captured in a photo as well. The idea of having a different photo for each medium must have been invented by photographers to make more money. Perhaps I am wrong, but I truly could care less what picture I have of you, as long as it is professionally taken and it looks like you.

CHAPTER 37

Daytime Actor Interviews

Since this book is for actors, I figured it would be interesting for you to hear the opinions of some young actors who have had success early in their careers. These are all actors I have cast on *Guiding Light*.

Aubrey Dollar

Aubrey Dollar (AD), until recently, played the role of Marina Cooper on *Guiding Light*. Her other credits include the pilot "Point Pleasant" for the Fox Network.

RD: How did you get started as an actor?

AD: My mom was an actor when I was growing up, so I would go to auditions with her, and then I started doing theatre in Raleigh, North Carolina, where I grew up.

RD: How do you prepare for your auditions?

AD: I think 95 percent of auditioning, because auditioning is very different from actually doing the job, is getting out of the way of yourself. I tend to usually try and trust and go with my initial instincts, because I think a lot of times, if you do that, you make strong choices and you stand out, and then if adjustments need to be made, you can make them. But if I prepare too much and then feel like I'm doing it totally wrong, I feel like I can't change it. So it's best to be free and see what happens.

RD: Do you think your instincts tend to be toward the simple choices or the more complicated choices?

AD: It varies. My instincts don't tend to be to stand up and throw a chair across the room. I guess they are on the simple side.

RD: In your experience, what has been the hardest thing for you about auditioning?

AD: A lot of times, it is that you are going in and reading with a casting director or an assistant or an intern and the scene is a love scene, and you're reading with a nineteen-year-old girl who is not really an actor, or the reader is someone who is completely monotone and you have eight people with little notepads writing things down as you are trying to emote or be in love with this person or cry. You read the scene and you realize that it is absolutely ridiculous. How am I going to do this in a room? I know that I can absolutely do this in the moment on the set, but how can I make this happen now and make it look believable?

RD: You are dealing with the limitations of the audition room?

AD: Absolutely, and caring what these people think.

RD: Have you ever felt that you tried to do too much in an audition?

AD: Yes, I think you need to be relaxed. Trying really hard comes across. I think that is a big thing that a lot of actors I know do, and what I did when I got out of theatre school is that you are trying so hard, you want this part so badly, and you come in the over-eager actor. You're giving all the right answers, and you're really happy and smiling, when really you are completely out of work, you are totally broke, your parents want you to move back home, everyone you know thinks what you're doing is stupid, you're in a horrible mood, you can't get any callbacks for any roles you're auditioning for, and you've been crying all morning. I find a lot of people will say to me that they booked their first role when they didn't want the part so much, because they let themselves be who they are.

RD: Did you do anything different for your *Guiding Light* audition compared to your non-daytime auditions?

AD: Yes. If you recall, I came in and my script was completely ripped because I had been sick and I was a wreck and I didn't feel like I was prepared properly. I had given up on daytime to this point. I had this thing where I refused to dress up a lot, like the other girls in their makeup and outfits, which annoyed me. So, I would go in with no makeup and dress down and would never get a callback, because I didn't want to play the game. I also didn't feel like myself when I did that.

RD: Do you think that game is less prevalent in primetime or in films?

AD: Yes, but I find myself doing it more now.

RD: There is a business side to every audition. . . .

AD: That's true.

RD: How important do you think it is for actors to have confidence when they are auditioning?

AD: Really important. But I don't think that confidence is always this gregarious, exuberant, fake put-on thing. I think confidence is being where you are, being comfortable with yourself, and trusting yourself and your skills.

RD: For your role on *Guiding Light*, you beat out hundreds of actors. Do you ever reflect on that?

AD: (*softly*) Yeah. It's a two-sided thing. A lot of times, every part I've ever gotten, I always thought it was some sort of fluke and somehow I fooled everyone. It doesn't make me feel like I'm better than all of them.

However, on the flip side, for my final audition for every role I've ever gotten, I've sort of had this energy—I guess this is the confidence thing you were talking about (it's also a great acting exercise to do in the waiting room)—but when I am sitting in the waiting room for my final audition, I've always gotten this kind of energy that is sort of like saying to myself, "This is mine, I'm getting this. It's none of yours, it is mine." I know that before I walk into the room. It's all about getting yourself to that mental place before you do it.

RD: I think there is a real quality to being confident, competitive, and lucky.

AD: Yes, absolutely.

RD: So, I think sometimes it's like: "Wow, I beat out hundreds of actors for this role, how fortunate am I? And also, how lucky am I?" But you have to be ready and good and make it happen.

AD: What you do in the room that instant is the thing. You can go in five minutes later, and for whatever reason, it will be totally different or much better or not as good. It is hit-or-miss.

RD: Or the casting director's perception of it could be totally different.

AD: Absolutely—it depends on who went in before you, too.

RD: Have you ever done anything in an audition that you later regretted?

AD: Yes, although it's mostly things I don't do that I regret. When I've had all these great ideas of the things I was going to do, and then I get in there and don't do them. I had a play audition and I was going to pace around the chair, if there was a chair there, because I always have issues about the chair. I'm always trying to decide if I'm going to use the chair and sit down if they are not taping me, or if I should move around a lot, and I always get mad when I wimp out and just end up sitting in the chair.

RD: And that maybe loses energy for you?

AD: Yeah, well, I just feel like the person who is going to get this role—even if what I did is fine—the person who is going to get this isn't just going to be sitting in the chair, or she is going to make it really compelling if she does.

RD: So the chair is an issue?

AD: It's awkward. It's especially awkward if there is no chair and you have to stand up and the person reading with you is sitting down. So it makes me wonder how I am going to physically interact during this audition.

I auditioned for The Crucible, which I really wanted. We're doing a scene with Abigail and John Proctor, and in the scene she's coming on to him very strongly, and the guy reading with me is sitting in a chair behind a table and they want me to stand, so it became very awkward to physicalize it if I didn't have a human being in front of me.

RD: Well, once again, the limitations of the room come into play. I think as an actor, when you are auditioning, you have to learn to play the emotional truth and the emotional result of the physical action, but saying that and doing that are two different things. It is not that easy to do.

AD: Absolutely.

RD: What advice do you have for any young actors who are starting their career and are just beginning the audition process?

AD: Don't put too much importance on it, because it is so arbitrary and you have to think that if you have one bad audition one day, there is always another day, or next week, to try something new.

Also, really push the limits. If there is something that scares you, do it and see what happens. I think if you make bold choices, then at least you will be remembered, because I think there is nothing worse than being mediocre and being like everyone else and having it be just okay. I think you have to let yourself be free and not be in your head.

RD: I agree. Good advice.

Jordi Vilasuso

Jordi Vilasuso (JV) received an Emmy for Outstanding Younger Actor in a Daytime Drama Series for his role as Tony Santos on *Guiding Light*. His other credits include the pilot *No Place Like Home* for the Fox Network.

RD: How did you get started as an actor?

JV: In the theatre. I started when I was young. It was my dream to see myself on stage or on the screen. I started with my junior high school drama club. My background is strong in the theatre but I eventually got my headshots done and started meeting agents. I had a monologue prepared to perform in their office. I think it is important that your monologue suits you. When you first meet people, you want to be able to show them what you can do, but you don't want to stretch too far.

RD: When you started meeting agents, did they ask you to do a monologue?

JV: Yes, especially when I moved to Los Angeles. I grew up in Miami. I had a two-minute monologue prepared.

RD: How do you prepare for your auditions?

JV: Well, if I get the script, I have to read the script. I think it's important because there are always clues for me about the character in the script. Also, I like to know the dialogue as well as possible because I don't want to be concerned with it.

I think it is important to find out as much as possible about the director, too. Now we have all these resources on the Internet, like *www.imdb.com*. I think you should look up the director and find out what he has done, watch his movies, and find out what his style is.

I also try and look to play against my type, which I think is a young, romantic leading man, but I try and downplay that as much as possible in the choices I make. Then I ask myself a lot of questions. I need to know why the character is in the scene and what I am doing in the scene. I also think about bringing props into the audition, if I think they can be helpful. The worst that can happen is the casting director is going to say, "No, just read with me." I make sure I try and listen in the reading. Listening is important; I learned that by working on *Guiding Light*.

Also, I think you need to come into the room with energy. You don't have to work the room, especially if the character is different from you. If you work the room, it then makes it harder to get back to what you prepared.

RD: In your experience, what has been the hardest thing for you about auditioning?

JV: Getting over the anxiety part of it. That's really the main thing. Basically, you are given a script and not given a lot of time with it. Also, if the casting director seems intimidating, you have to not let that bring you down. Casting directors are human. They do the same things you do in their lives; they've gone through the same things you've gone through. I think it helps to remind yourself of that. I think having the lines down helps, too.

RD: So you like being memorized?

JV: I do. I don't like looking at the script during an audition. A lot of people I know use the script, though. But, for me, it is more difficult and I feel less confident if I don't know the words. I feel like I can't perform and listen if I am constantly looking at the script and then looking up at the reader.

RD: I think it is valuable that you say that, because I think people do have different opinions about that. Certain actors have to be memorized and some actors don't want to be, so I think it is about finding what works for you.

So dealing with audition anxiety had been an issue. Do you feel like you still deal with that now?

JV: I think it is always going to be there, but I think you can use it to your advantage. You see, I am such a perfectionist, so I try and not judge myself. That is the worst thing you can do in an audition.

RD: Have you ever felt that you tried to do too much in an audition?

JV: No, not really. I think if you do too much, they can always tell you to tone it down. I think you need to give as much of yourself as possible. I'm really against lazy acting and an "I don't care" attitude. Of course you care—your character is dealing with conflict and he cares about that. People respect you if you can give as much as possible.

RD: I think what you are saying is great. I always say that there is nothing about the audition that is not important. The fact that someone has chosen this scene for the audition tells you that the character and the actor cannot be lazy about it.

Did you do anything different for your *Guiding Light* audition compared to your non-daytime auditions?

JV: The thing about this role was that it worked out very well in terms of what was going on in my life at that time. I was nineteen and not that experienced. I was just getting used to living on the West Coast, but thinking about moving to New York and working on this character seemed like a great opportunity.

One of the things that helped me was that for the screen test, I wasn't anxious. People say when you want something, you don't get it. You get what you need, not what you want. So, the fact that I did get it was great. I don't think my test was the best thing I ever did, but it got me the part—thanks to you. I was excited about the character and I embraced it.

RD: You were young, so you may not have had any attitude about it, but did you say to yourself, "This is a soap," so that you would approach it in a different way—different than a film or prime-time audition?

JV: No, I approached it as a job. If you approach it as a soap, then you are putting a label on it. Do you think there is a size issue in the performance of it? Less is more?

RD: I think there may be a performance issue due to the technology and shooting style on a given set. I don't think there is an audition difference.

How important do you think it is for actors to have confidence when they are auditioning?

JV: Definitely you need a lot of confidence. That does not mean being cocky. The people who are making the decisions have to know that this actor cares about doing good work. That is the most important thing—the passion. Just make sure you don't fall into the trap of cockiness. Be passionate as an artist and an actor; show them that you care.

RD: For your role on *Guiding Light* and, for that matter, the pilot you did, you beat out hundreds of actors for those roles. Do you ever reflect on that?

JV: I try not to think about it. I think it's great and I'm proud, but it's just the tip of the iceberg. Now that you've got the role, you have to push yourself even harder. I come from a work ethic knowing that there is always going to be someone who wants it more. So you always have to be on top of your game. You have to find ways to always make it interesting. Be passionate about the work. But getting the job is a great feeling.

RD: Have you ever done anything in an audition that you later regretted?

JV: Yeah, I can remember being anxious and I have been a victim of lazy acting. Maybe I shut down when I am dealing with the anxiety.

RD: What advice do you have for any young actors who are starting their careers and are just beginning the audition process?

JV: Get into acting class now and look for a teacher who is really going to push you. Be honest about the character and the role and the story. You have to do the work to give a good performance. Also, don't beat yourself up, because rejection is tough. You're an artist; you have to keep the passion and realize that it isn't going to happen overnight.

Daniel Cosgrove

Daniel Cosgrove (DC) plays the role of Bill Lewis on *Guiding Light*. Previous credits include Matt Durning on *Beverly Hills, 90210*, Scott Chandler on *All My Children*, and Richard Bagg in *National Lampoon's Van Wilder*.

RD: How did you get started as an actor?

DC: At the end of high school, I started looking into colleges that had good theatre programs, and in my second semester I took an improvisational technique class, and that is when I knew I fell in love with it. After that, I did a one-act play, and then I decided it was something I wanted to pursue. It wasn't until a few years later that I followed through with it.

However, when I was really young, I barely spoke because I was very, very shy. I was very uncomfortable speaking, all the way up until first grade. In kindergarten, my teacher told my mother that she knew I could speak, but had never heard me talk. I always received an "N" for "needs improvement" for class participation, and I was assigned to the lowest-level reading group. However, the class did scenes for Thanksgiving that year for all the parents and other students. I remember the class getting all dressed up like pilgrims and Native Americans. I remember getting a lot of responses, and I realized I was able to make people laugh, and that brought me out of my shell. By the end of the year, I was in the first reading group; I had made a huge leap. I look back now at that and realize how important acting has been in my life. Through humor, I was able to communicate, and that is what is important to me—if I can make people laugh.

RD: That is a great story.

DC: Yeah, by third grade, I was winning spelling bee contests.

RD: Let's talk about now. How do you prepare for your auditions?

DC: It depends. A lot of auditions are different. Sometimes you get sides the day of, sometimes the night before, and sometimes you have them the whole weekend before the audition. So my preparation is based on how much time I have and what kind of piece it is. If it is a comedy, it is all about the timing, the pacing, and the rhythm of it.

RD: Is there a rhythm to a dramatic scene?

DC: It is actually what I look for in all auditions. I realize there is a reason why my character is there and why they chose this scene. I look at it like a puzzle with a lot of pieces to it. You have to look at who you are and the relationship to the other person. The who, what, and why. Ask yourself a lot of questions. I like to go through the dialogue once or twice and then kind of run through my lines. I even like to embellish on my own during my rehearsal time so I can find the ups and downs in the scene, all the levels and layers to it.

I like to experiment with the lines, doing them backwards, in crazy voices, trying to pull out of it as much as I can. I do this so I can get comfortable with what is on the page. I like to strip it down and then go back to what is on the page.

RD: Is that a long process? Are you able to still do it when you do not have a lot of time to prepare?

DC: I still do it. Initially, when I started out, I was so concerned about saying the words in a way a person really talks. For me, just me, I like to find what is underneath it all. But if I just concentrate on saying the lines only, then I am not looking for what is underneath it all, and it sounds so scripted.

RD: Do you ad-lib?

DC: When I am rehearsing, but after that, I get back to what is on the page. It helps me prepare.

RD: There is a difference between auditioning and performing.

DC: Right. In a performance, things can change because of the person you are working with. In an audition, you know going in that nine out of ten times there will be a reader that you will not be getting a lot from. So that is why I like to get as much as I can out of it, and then get back to the page and the words.

RD: Auditioning is about you. If you rely on a reader, that's a problem.

DC: That's exactly why I work out the character, and have the page in my hand so I don't get lost. For me, I like bringing as much through improvisation as possible to draw upon while I'm in the room.

RD: In your experience, what has been the hardest thing for you about auditioning?

DC: Keeping my mouth shut. It's about going in and doing the job and leaving. All casting directors are different, producers are different. Some want to get right to it, and I always have to remember that I am there to do a job. Some like to say hi, have a little chitchat, and then get to it. As an actor, you ask yourself, Should I be more open? Should I have talked more? Should I have tried to be more personable? Should I have asked more questions? You can ask yourself a hundred and one questions, but I just think you have to be prepared and do the best you can by knowing your work and just trying to bring something to it. Who knows what they want when you walk in the door that day?

RD: The chance that you are what they are looking for is not in your favor, so you might as well enjoy it.

DC: You could completely think you are not right for this role, but you should not worry about that. You should just go in and try and make an impression of being able to do the work. Because you can go in there . . . I've been in situations where I've auditioned for one character and didn't get it, but did get another role. Bring what you can, be prepared, because you never know. You might not get a job. Then again, you might not get *that* job, and they may give you another one, or they could bring you in for something else.

RD: How important do you think it is for an actor to have confidence when he is auditioning?

DC: I think it is very important that you act like you have confidence.

(We laugh.)

RD: That's a good answer.

DC: There are a lot of people who may lack confidence for various reasons, whether it is about playing the role, or if you haven't had enough time to prepare. But if you go in and just have fun, be comfortable enough to know you can get the job done. If a lack of confidence makes you timid, then that's not very interesting.

RD: For your roles on *Guiding Light, All My Children,* and *Beverly Hills, 90210,* you beat out hundreds of actors for those parts. Do you ever reflect on that?

DC: Wow, what pressure. I better get my lines down today. That's great, but there's another actor getting off the bus that is new in town who wants your role, and that's just the name of the game. As an actor, you are constantly asking yourself, Why are you putting yourself through this humiliation, but you must have confidence to pursue this job. You have to believe that you have something to offer, and you should remember that every time you get into an audition room. Don't think about the actors auditioning, don't worry about if the other person is better looking or funnier—you can't think of that. You can't think, "There are hundreds of people auditioning. I will never get the job."

RD: Have you ever done anything in an audition that you later regretted?

DC: A lot of things. There are times when I wished I didn't talk so much or ramble or try and be so funny. There is nothing worse than leaving an audition and feeling like you didn't give what you could give. You have to go for it. The first audition I ever had was for *Guiding Light*, and I left thinking I nailed it. I did what I wanted to do, and when my agent got feedback, the casting director said that I was "unfocused and rushed," and here I was, walking away thinking I nailed it. However, five auditions later, I went in at *All My Children* and didn't get the role, but they offered me something else. I was too young for the first role.

RD: Your callback from that first audition was the opportunity they gave you for the new role. That came directly from the first audition.

DC: I learned from my first audition that I was not listening and participating in the scene, and I was so concerned about the feedback.

RD: Perception is an amazing thing. An actor could think he had a lousy audition and then he gets a callback.

RD: What advice do you have for any young actors who are starting their career and are just beginning the audition process?

DC: Actors starting out should first take a good acting class. The first time I took a class, it was a summer program at the Lee Strasberg Institute, and I remember on my way there thinking,

"I don't need classes. All you have to do is make the lines real."
And when I got to the class, I was nervous and realized there is
a lot to learn. I realize now that I will continue to learn. I walk
out of here [Guiding Light] learning something. You learn on a
continuous basis and you shouldn't be close-minded. Don't
think you know. We have to study and be open-minded. You
have to keep yourself open to criticism and try to learn from it.
You can't get defensive when you are learning this business and
craft. You can't feel like you have all the answers. You have to
stay open to someone else's feedback and perspective of it, but
it's your judgment of that feedback that counts.

CHAPTER 38

Agent and Manager Interviews

Although this book is about auditioning and the relationship to the casting director, I thought it might be interesting for you to hear the opinions of some talent agents and managers and learn what their take is on the subject of auditioning and on the relationship with the casting director. I am also assuming that many young actors reading this book might be without representation, and it has been my experience that those actors without representation are consumed with the notion of trying to get some. I do understand this need, and perhaps this will give you some insight into an agent's job.

Michael Bruno

Michael Bruno (MB) is a personal manager who specializes in daytime television.

RD: How important do you feel it is for your clients to have a solid audition technique?

MB: Very important. Auditioning and acting, once you have the job, are two different animals. If you don't know how to audition, you can't get the job.

RD: What is the single most significant piece of advice you can give your clients about professionalism and auditioning?

MB: Be prepared and don't ask stupid questions. I always feel it's important for you, the actor, to end the interview, without being rude, of course. Leave the casting people/agents with a sense of them wanting you more, rather than overstaying your welcome. No idle chitchatting.

RD: How hard is it for you when you know that you have an actor who is very right for a role, and the feedback is negative after he has his audition for that role?

MB: The biggest thing for actors to know is when they did a good job at an audition and when they did a bad job. I don't care if an actor calls and tells me that he really blew it. That's fine. Everybody has a bad day. What makes me very nervous is when an actor says how great he was, and the casting director/agent has just the opposite to say.

RD: Is that the casting director's fault or the actor's fault?

MB: The casting people want you to be great. They want you to get the role so they can go home or move on to the next role, so it's the actor's fault. Actors have this weird feeling that casting people are not on their side, which makes absolutely no sense.

RD: Do you encourage your clients to get training and keep studying the craft of acting?

MB: Yes. It's like going to the gym. When actors sign with me and say, "Okay, what do I do on my end?" I say, go to the gym and go to acting class. I don't care who you study with, but I want to be able to know in my heart when I'm pitching clients that they are getting better as actors every day, without me having to check in on them.

RD: Do you ever work with your clients before their auditions? If yes, why? If no, why not?

MB: Yes, almost always. Especially the younger ones. I want to see what they come up with and steer them in the right direction. I also feel that if you're walking into an audition, you're walking in with my name and reputation, so if you suck, then I suck. AND I DON'T SUCK!

RD: What is the key to a sustained career as an actor? Not a famous career, but what does it take to be a working actor?

MB: Work begets work. The second one starts thinking about doing or not doing a project because of money or fame, you're in trouble. Doing a small play in the boondocks could lead to a movie. You never know. I always say, take any work offered to you, because it's meant to bring you to the next place, not only in your acting career, but in your life.

Jill McGrath

Jill McGrath (JM) is a talent agent in the theatrical division at the Abrams Artists Agency in New York.

RD: How important do you feel it is for your clients to have a solid audition technique?

JM: I think it is very important for my clients to have a solid audition technique. Often, an actor is only given five minutes when auditioning for a role. Technique creates focus and the ability to combat nerves, which makes your chances of booking the job that much greater.

RD: What is the single most significant piece of advice you can give your clients about professionalism and auditioning?

JM: The biggest piece of advice I can give an actor is to be prepared. Preparation is everything. Keep in mind when you go to an audition that even if you don't get the part, if you come prepared, a casting director will almost always bring you in for another role or a different project that you might be better suited for.

RD: How hard is it for you when you know that you have an actor who is very right for a role, and the feedback is negative after he has his audition for that role?

JM: When I receive negative feedback on a client after an audition, it is obviously very disappointing, especially knowing that the actor is more than capable. I will usually talk to my clients and see how they think the audition went, to make sure everyone is on the same page. If they felt badly about it, knowing they could have done better, then we can chalk it up to a bad day—everyone has them. This also gives me the opportunity to call the casting director to explain and do some damage control. If the actor felt good about the audition despite the negative feedback, I would then discuss the process, explain that what the actor did in the room did not play out the way he intended it to, and talk about what steps he needs to take in order to "fix" the problem.

RD: Is that the casting director's fault or the actor's fault?

JM: Unfortunately, the blame will usually land on the actor. This is why having a solid audition technique is crucial, and will often protect the actor from receiving negative feedback.

RD: Do you encourage your clients to get training and keep studying the craft of acting?

JM: In order to stay competitive in this business, you need to train and continue to work on your craft at all times.

RD: Do you ever work with your clients before their auditions? If yes, why? If no, why not?

JM: I usually do not work with my clients before auditions. I am too busy pitching them for future opportunities. I usually leave that to an acting coach or their manager, who will most likely have the time to help prepare an actor for each individual audition.

RD: What is the key to a sustained career as an actor? Not a famous career, but what does it take to be a working actor?

JM: There are a couple of factors that go into a successful acting career, with talent being the most important. Some others are skill, preparation, representation, and a positive attitude.

Rhonda Price

Rhonda Price (RP) is the Senior Vice President of Talent at the Gersh Agency in New York.

RD: How important do you feel it is for your clients to have a solid audition technique?

RP: For the most part, I find this is extremely important. An actor has to be able to perform at a certain level in a room to get the job, especially as the stakes get higher with major feature film parts, television leads, and coveted theatre parts. If one is nervous or feeling "blocked," technique gives one the added confidence to hopefully move through it. An actor can be a bit off, but with technique, the person watching it doesn't need to know! Besides, other actors going up for the part who have that training will show it in the room; it can make all the difference. It also teaches one consistency. But I must say, I also represent people who are quite young or who started working out of the gate and didn't take an audition technique class. Some just know how to tap into that special area of themselves.

RD: What is the single most significant piece of advice you can give your clients about professionalism and auditioning?

RP: Be on time, be prepared, look the best you can, and own the room without being rude or arrogant. It's hard enough to audition—to be in a situation to be judged. Don't go into that room with a strike against you, where you have control.

RD: How hard is it for you when you know that you have an actor who is very right for a role, and the feedback is negative after he has his audition for that role?

RP: Extremely. First, I ask the client how HE feels he did. I want to see if he feels the same way, or feels he did a great job. I always take into consideration what the feedback is and who it is from, as well. There are times when a casting director says lovely things to the actor in the room, and then calls me with a completely differing opinion. I think it is important to have a bead on what happens in the room with your client, but also to acknowledge you are not in there with him, so it's really about making sure he is present in the room and doing his best work. In the end, I say to my clients, "As long as you have done your very best, and you have no regrets as to those five or ten minutes or half hour in the room, you have won." But I won't lie—I do get frustrated . . . I want my clients to work!

RD: Is that the casting director's fault or the actor's fault?

RP: It can be both. If a client is not prepared, it's his fault. If it is an adjustment that can be given and is not, then I think that is the casting director's job. If the casting director gives a note and the actor doesn't fully realize it, that's a toss-up. Sometimes actors need time to process, and sometimes they can take it in and process it right away. That goes back to technique—being in the moment and feeling secure and listening.

RD: Do you encourage your clients to get training and keep studying the craft of acting?

RP: ABSOLUTELY. We are all students of what we do. There is always something to learn and explore. Many of my most successful clients are the ones who are still in class. I often chuckle at those that feel they did a year or two in a conservatory or have a Master's degree, and think that is enough. Actors feed off of other actors. Actors learn when working and when not working. It extends beyond actual class and private coaching. It's about expanding your knowledge via books, old movies, theatre, dance, music, politics . . . and most importantly, working on your inner self. It's all about tapping into that place in yourself that makes your work full and unique to you.

RD: Do you ever work with your clients before their auditions? If yes, why? If no, why not?

RP: I do. I work with a lot of my clients in our tape room, so I know them and they know me. It gives them the chance to work aloud, and they know my comments come out of love and respect and a desire for them to get the job. I always say, "I AM NOT AN ACTOR; I HAVE NEVER TAKEN A CLASS," but I know what it feels like to be affected by someone. Let's do the scene; affect me. Some clients hate it—makes them nervous!

RD: What is the key to a sustained career as an actor? Not a famous career, but what does it take to be a working actor?

RP: I wish there was an answer for that—I'd feel like I had the keys to the kingdom of the acting G–d. To me, I think it is about knowing that like anything in life, it's cyclical. You can't be on top every moment of your career. But when you are good, when you have a talent that the world responds to, have faith. And always work on your personal self. Growth in one's brain and soul deepens work as much as "acting like you are a tree" . . . not that there is not value in that exercise! But most of all, if the process and the work still give you the joy and a satisfaction, and you still have the undying passion of not wanting to do anything else, that's a big part of it. We all have different thresholds for pain and gain, and for what is a successful, sustained career.

CHAPTER 39

Casting Director Interviews

I thought it would be valuable to hear the perspectives of some of my peers. I have asked three top casting directors whom I know and respect to share their thoughts about auditioning. It is my hope that some of the things they say will complement as well as contradict what I have said. It is imperative that you have many people's opinions for you to determine what your own is.

Mary Clay Boland

Mary Clay Boland (MCB) is the Emmy-nominated casting director for the daytime television program As the World Turns.

RD: What are some of the most important qualities you are looking for in actors when they are auditioning?

MCB: I am looking for a great look, someone appealing and charismatic and charming. I also look for intelligence and training. The look varies with the role. I also want an actor who makes choices and understands the character and what his motivations are.

RD: How important is it for you to see that an actor has clearly prepared for his audition?

MCB: It is very important. That is your first impression of the actor. If actors come in unprepared, I feel as though they are not responsible actors, and I would be afraid to trust them. If you are serious about acting, an audition should be your number one priority.

RD: Do you have a different perception of actors who have training compared to actors who do not? I guess my question is, How important is their acting training to you?

MCB: Training is very important to me in adult actors. It is not the only thing; instinct and natural talent play a large role as well. I feel more secure going with actors who have a lot of training. This does not just include school. Experience can be a form of training as well. If someone has done a lot of work but does not have a theatre degree, I still consider that training. However, it can be a catch-22, because if someone has not got experience, they may find it harder to get the first job. I would always pick an actor with training over someone who has none.

As far as children go, training is not important. Children either get it or they do not. The most important thing to look for in children is how comfortable they are around strangers, how smart they are, and if they want to be there.

RD: In your career as a casting director, have you ever been excited about an actor for a role, and then when he got the role, been disappointed by his performance? No names, please.

MCB: Yes, I have. You never know if someone is great in the audition room if that will translate on set or stage once he gets with the rest of the cast. Some people are better in an audition than when actually working. That is just a risk you have to take. Recasting is a major part of casting, and every actor should know that. Booking a job is huge, but keeping a job can be harder.

RD: What do you think went wrong?

MCB: Sometimes in daytime drama, it is memorizing all the scripts. You work at a fast pace in daytime, and some people cannot handle that. Sometimes it is chemistry between the actor and the leading man or woman, and sometimes it is just that the director or producer decided to take the character in a different direction once the character has been fleshed out a little. It can be very random, so it is best not to take it personally.

RD: What do you think is the hardest thing about auditioning, from the actor's perspective?

MCB: It is a very anxiety-ridden experience. The actor can just make the choices he thinks are best and hope they are what the casting director or director has in mind. I think it is the lack of control that is difficult. All the actor can do is go in, do his best, and hope it is a fit.

RD: How about from the casting director's perspective?

MCB: The casting director has to figure out what the producers, director, and writers all pictured for the role. There can be eight actors who read beautifully for the role, but only one may have the look they wanted. The casting director has to figure out which one they want. We also see a lot of people at once; after seeing fifty people, the fifty-first person is difficult to figure out unless he blows you away with his audition.

RD: Give me a few things that actors do that drive you crazy. Let this be the opportunity to advise young actors on what not to do in an audition.

MCB: NEVER come in the room in front of the director and producers and announce that you are "not right for this role, but came in anyway so you could meet them." If the casting director brought you in, then she knows something you don't. If you do not think you are right for a role, either pass on it or ask the casting director about it and tell her your doubts. This way, the casting director can tell you why she thinks you are right. This statement immediately pisses off producers and makes them feel like their time is being wasted.

Also, BE PREPARED. I don't care if you shot a commercial all night, or some indie film, or had a modeling job. If you are not prepared, do not come in with excuses and waste my time.

Also, AVOID PROPS.

RD: What are some positive audition pointers you can give to some young actors who are starting their career?

MCB: Dress nice. You do not have to be formal, but do not come to an audition looking like you just woke up. Only superstars can get away with that. Also, like I said above, be prepared; make some choices about the scene. If you have questions, feel free to ask them, but you should have a good idea of what you want to do before you walk in. Also, be on time. It is scary to hire an actor who never shows up for an audition on time.

Marnie Saitta

Marnie Saitta (MS) is the casting director for the daytime television program *The Young and the Restless*.

RD: What are some of the most important qualities you are looking for in an actor when he is auditioning?

MS: Confidence and commitment. The ability to be confident in the choices and the work he has done in the development of his character, and the commitment to follow through on those choices, really set actors apart.

RD: How important is it for you to see that an actor has clearly prepared for his audition?

MS: Being prepared is a necessity for actors. This is not to be confused with merely knowing one's dialogue. Being prepared consists of character and scene work. Many times, actors are auditioning with material that gives them limited background on the character. In order to be fully prepared, an actor must do the work to develop the character and the background of the character to make the scene truthful and rich, not just one-dimensional. Being off book is not required, but having a firm grasp of the dialogue gives the actor more freedom and confidence to make strong choices and makes him spend less time worrying about the next line.

RD: Do you have a different perception of actors who have training compared to actors who do not? I guess my question is, How important is their acting training to you?

MS: An actor who has training definitely conveys the message that he respects and takes his craft seriously. There is a level of commitment there that definitely gets my respect right off the bat. An actor who studies usually has more confidence to take bigger risks in a scene and commit to a choice. Even the most naturally gifted actors must study. Natural talent is nurtured and challenged throughout an actor's training.

RD: In your career as a casting director, have you ever been excited about an actor for a role, and then when he got the role, you were disappointed by his performance? No names, please.

MS: Not that often, but it definitely has happened.

RD: What do you think went wrong?

MS: In the few times it has happened with a contract actor, the three-camera blocking technique and the amount of material in a day's work proved to be the biggest challenges. An actor can be great in the room during the audition because he has a number of days to rehearse the scene and the blocking is usually minimal. Once the actor starts his day-to-day routine, the blocking gets more intricate and the amount of material increases, and an actor can lose the ability to maintain the commitment to the scene because he gets too focused on remembering the dialogue and the blocking. Most actors need a short amount of time to get used to this process, but for a few it can prove to be too much. Daytime is a phenomenal place for an actor to develop really great habits, but, conversely, an actor in daytime can also develop some bad habits by taking shortcuts and getting lazy about how much commitment he puts toward a scene. That is always a big disappointment to see.

There have been a few times where we have hired day players who are great during the audition, but find themselves overwhelmed down on the set and let their nerves get the best of them.

RD: What do you think is the hardest thing about auditioning, from the actor's perspective?

MS: Learning to relax and be confident in what most actors consider to be a nerve-racking process. I think that actors do their best work in their living rooms, with no one around and where they feel completely uninhibited. During the auditioning process, inhibitions are an actor's worst enemy, because they can squash an actor's instinct and the confidence to trust those instincts. Things that I think add to the nervousness an actor can feel are the thought that he will only have one shot at nailing a scene, the lack of information an actor has about the character, and the general feeling of being judged.

RD: How about from the casting director's perspective?

MS: The hardest part about my job is also the part that I love the most, which is finding an actor who breathes life into a role in a way you never imagined, and who also fits the image that the show is looking for. I am always faced with the question, "Do you have to be gorgeous to be on a soap?" An actor who is considered "gorgeous" can "lose" his looks quickly in the room if he can't act. Conversely, if an actor is what some consider to be average looking, but is an amazing talent, he can make you believe he is sexy and gorgeous in his performance.

RD: Give me a few things that actors do that drive you crazy. Let this be the opportunity to advise young actors on what not to do in an audition.

MS: 1. Not being prepared or seeming lackadaisical in the commitment to the scene.

2. Making excuses as to why they are not prepared before they begin a scene.

3. Being late for an appointment.

4. Headshots that look far better than the actor in person.

5. Having their head in the paper throughout the whole scene.

6. Touching the casting director in the scene.

RD: What are some positive audition pointers you can give to some young actors who are starting their career?

MS: First of all, the actor needs to understand that casting directors and actors are on the same team. Actors have a perception that casting directors are the Big Bad Wolf, but the reality is that casting directors need the actors just as much as they need us. Actors are the casting director's body of work, and without you, we cannot do our job.

Second, gather as much information as you can about the character from the material that you are given, and then do the work to fill in the missing pieces so you can create a multi-dimensional, rich character.

Third, know your material, but never put your sides down in the audition. It is not required that you be off book, so don't put the added extra pressure on yourself.

Last, study, study, study. Respect your craft and challenge yourself in class, and it will show in your auditions.

Andra Reeve-Rabb

Andra Reeve-Rabb (ARR) is the Director of Primetime Casting at CBS in New York.

RD: What are some of the most important qualities you are looking for in an actor when he is auditioning?

ARR: The ability to come in with choices made for the character, but then being ready to throw the homework out and being able to take direction on the spot.

RD: How important is it for you to see that an actor has clearly prepared for his audition?

ARR: It's everything! I feel that it is incredibly important for an actor to mine the material for everything and to be very familiar with it, but to not feel the pressure to memorize. We assume that when you get the job, you can memorize your lines. It is important to know it well enough to connect with the person you are reading with and make full eye contact, but not get caught up in the memorization. Be present and in the moment instead of trying to remember what comes next.

RD: Do you have a different perception of actors who have training compared to actors who do not? I guess my question is, How important is their acting training to you?

ARR: I feel that it is an actor's responsibility to train his/her whole life. Never stop taking classes or working with a coach.

RD: In your career as a casting director, have you ever been excited about an actor for a role, and then when he got the role, you were disappointed by his performance? No names, please.

ARR: Yes. Some actors are great auditioners; they have mastered the art of the audition but then that's it! It doesn't go deeper or further than that initial audition, and they just don't ultimately deliver on set.

RD: What do you think is the hardest thing about auditioning, from the actor's perspective?

ARR: I think the hardest thing for an actor is just getting past the nerves. There is sort of an "us versus them" concept that I think is so important to let go of when you go in for an audition. It would be great for actors and casting directors to recognize that we are all in this together. We need you as much as you need us.

RD: How about from the casting director's perspective?

ARR: Giving each actor his time. When you see two actors every fifteen minutes for six hours, it is important to keep up your energy and remind yourself that you have to give the last actor of the day the same amount of energy and interest that you gave the first actor of the day.

RD: Give me a few things that actors do that drive you crazy. Let this be the opportunity to advise young actors on what not to do in an audition.

ARR: Use common sense. The simple things: be on time, be prepared, and relax and enjoy yourself. Your audition starts the second you enter the building; how you treat everyone from the security guard to your fellow actors is a reflection of you. Know your audience. If I am a casting director for television, why would you tell me that you don't like TV and don't on principle even own a TV!

RD: What are some positive audition pointers you can give to some young actors who are starting their career?

ARR: Relax, get rid of the nerves; they are your worst enemy. Go into the audition knowing that we want you to get the part! If you get the part, then our work is done! Come into the audition with as much information as you can. That is an important part of your job. It is your responsibility to keep up with the latest theatre, film, and television shows. You don't want to go into an audition for *CSI: Miami* having not seen the show before, and therefore not knowing the tone and style of the series.

CHAPTER 40

The Workbook

Now, for the majority of this book, I have preached to forget about the audition after the audition. The philosophical outlook I want you to have is that you are not going to book the job, so go in and do your work, be prepared, be professional and gracious. I still believe that, but now that you are almost finished with this book, I want you to try the technique for your next twenty-five auditions, and I want you to keep track of those twenty-five auditions. After those initial twenty-five auditions of applying the technique, you will have a better understanding of the technique and whether all or any part of it will work for you.

So, we are going to make a workbook to help you keep track of those twenty-five auditions. I still don't want you to obsess about the audition in terms of "will you book the job or not"; that is not the objective here. The objective is to monitor your progress for educational purposes.

Make the Workbook

The first thing you need to do is to go out and buy a very large three-ring binder to hold 8.5-by-11-inch paper, a three-hole punch, and twenty-five page dividers. Take each divider and on the tab, write down "Audition #1," "Audition #2," and so on, until you have completed all twenty-five. Then, I want you to go to a computer or just use a notepad (8.5-by-11-inch paper) and write out the following on a single piece of paper, spaced out so you have room for answers:

PROGRAM:
CASTING DIRECTOR:
ADDRESS OF AUDITION:
AUDITIONING FOR ROLE OF:
DATE:

You will make twenty-five copies of this piece of paper and insert it behind each divider in your binder.

Write Down the Questions

Then, on separate pages, I want you to write out the following questions, leaving space for your answers. Use as many sheets of paper as needed.

1. Did you break the scene down into beats?
2. How many beat changes did you have?
3. Do you feel like you identified all of the beat changes?
4. Do you feel like you inserted too many beat changes?
5. List the subject words for all your beats:
6. List the feeling words for all your beats:
7. Do you think you successfully played the feelings of the beats as they related to the subject of the beats?
8. Did you identify the major beat change?
9. At what line was the major beat change introduced?
10. What was your character's major objective?
11. Do you feel like you played your major objective?
12. Did your character achieve or not achieve the major objective?
13. Do you feel like you successfully played the major beat change moment?
14. Did you dictate the pace of the audition?
15. Did you raise the stakes and have a sense of urgency during the audition?
16. Did you sit or stand during the audition?
17. Was the audition taped?
18. Were you professional at the audition?
19. Now that it is over, would you have changed any of your choices?
20. Did anything unexpected happen in the audition?
21. How was your focus?
22. How was your level of confidence?
23. Do you feel like you were able to apply the technique in this audition?
24. How do you feel the audition went? Excellent? Good? Average? Fair? Poor?

25. Have you received any feedback on the audition? If yes, what feedback?
26. Did you receive a callback for this audition?
27. Did you send a thank-you postcard or note to the casting director yet? (optional)

Make another twenty-five copies of these questions and insert them behind each divider and underneath the previous information-al page you have already created and inserted in the binder. It is important to do this all at once, and not wait until every audition has happened. If you really want to track your progress, then it is best to have the workbook binder already created, so that you only have to fill it in and not produce it every time. My fear is that you will not track your progress due to frustration and the additional effort it will require to make the binder after every audition. Do it early and be done with it.

Track Your Progress

Now this is simple. All you have to do is after every audition take the sides, three-hole punch them, and insert them in your binder behind the first page and on top of the questions. Then, fill out the question forms that you have created. The top form will track the project you auditioned for, the role, who the casting director was, and the address of the audition. This is informational stuff. The last set of questions is vital to track your progress. You need to honestly answer these questions. Be reflective on your preparation, your choices, and the actual in-the-room audition. Your sides should be written on, and if you had any additional notes or pages from your preparation, you can include them in the workbook as well.

As you continue to receive auditions, keep adding to the workbook in date order of the audition. From time to time, look back at some of the earlier choices that you made, and the feelings you had after the audition, to monitor your progress. I think this will be a great, organized and fun way to track your development. Don't let yourself be frustrated by the process and by the potential for a lack of progress. Remind yourself that you knew you were not going to book the jobs anyway, and that this is just for your own education.

I am not suggesting that this technique will be mastered in twenty-five auditions. For some actors this technique may come easily, and for others it could take several years and many, many auditions, and for still others it may not be a useful tool. For others, there may only be a point or two of the technique that, combined with their current process and acting training, allows them to succeed beyond their current status.

Sample Workbook Submission

Below, please find an example of how an actress could fill out the workbook forms if she had an audition for the woman in the audition scene used throughout this book:

SAMPLE WORKBOOK FORM
PROGRAM: *Guiding Light*
CASTING DIRECTOR: Rob Decina
ADDRESS OF AUDITION: 44th Street, New York, NY
AUDITIONING FOR ROLE OF: Woman
DATE: 8/9/2003

1. Did you break the scene down into beats?
   Yes.
2. How many beat changes did you have?
   Three.
3. Do you feel like you identified all of the beat changes?
   Yes.
4. Do you feel like you inserted too many beat changes?
   No. I feel confident that I identified all of the beat changes. If I had any more, it would have been too much.
5. List the subject words for all your beats:
   Beat #1: food
   Beat #2: bowling
   Beat #3: Luigi's
   Beat #4: affair
6. List the feeling words for all your beats:
   A: Beat #1: annoyed
   Beat #2: hopeful
   Beat #3: insulted
   Beat #4: confident

7. Do you think you successfully played the feelings of the beats as they related to the subject of the beats?
Yes. I was happy with all my choices and the relationship of the subject word to the feeling word in the beats.

8. Did you identify the major beat change?
Yes.

9. At what line was the major beat change introduced?
"Because I saw you and your girlfriend there! I know you've been cheating on me."

10. What was your character's major objective?
To confront my husband about his affair.

11. Do you feel like you played your major objective?
Yes.

12. Did your character achieve or not achieve the major objective?
Achieved the major objective.

13. Do you feel like you successfully played the major beat change moment?
Yes, absolutely.

14. Did you dictate the pace of the audition?
I think so. Perhaps I could have been stronger to respond and pick up my cues in the opening beat, allowing me to be in a little more control.

15. Did you raise the stakes and have a sense of urgency during the audition?
Yes. I was clear about that after the first beat.

16. Did you sit or stand during the audition?
I stood. I wanted the energy of being on my feet.

17. Was the audition taped?
No, it was not.

18. Were you professional at the audition?
Of course, and gracious, too.

19. Now that it is over, would you have changed any of your choices?
I think my feeling word in beat number three ("insulted") was the right choice, but I do not think that I fully embodied that feeling in that beat. This made for a hard transition into the final beat.

20. Did anything unexpected happen in the audition?
The casting director was an excellent reader! Seriously, I found that I was listening very clearly in the audition.

21. How was your focus?

    My focus was good. I didn't do anything that was distracting. I stayed in place and didn't have any props.

22. How was your level of confidence?

    I could have been a little more confident in my choices and myself.

23. Do you feel like you were able to apply the technique in this audition?

    I would say that I am 85 percent there.

24. How do you feel the audition went? Excellent? Good? Average? Fair? Poor?

    Good.

25. Have you received any feedback on the audition? If yes, what feedback?

    My agent told me that the casting director liked me, but didn't think I was right for the role. He said he would keep me in mind for other roles.

26. Did you receive a callback for this audition?

    No. [This can be updated later if it changes.]

27. Did you send a thank-you postcard or note to the casting director yet? (optional)

    Yes.

CHAPTER 41

Final Advice

The television audition is the single moment that most reflects where the craft of acting meets the business of trying to get an acting job. I am fortunate enough to witness this crucial junction on a daily basis. Sometimes that event is staggeringly successful, and many times, it goes horribly wrong. Now that you have read this book, you are in a wonderful position to try out this experience firsthand.

Your Obligation and Commitment

If you are serious about pursuing a career, then you must accept the enormous obligation that is in front of you. It is a great burden that you are taking on. It is my opinion that when you decide you want to pursue an acting career, you have an obligation to hold up your end of the bargain. Your end is the commitment. You must promise yourself that you will work hard and study hard, while remaining humble and eager. You must promise to make every effort to strive for the level of success and commitment that every successful actor before you has strived for, and at the same time raise the bar of your own standards for yourself and for every other actor who follows you. You must make a commitment to keep studying and learning and observing. You must promise to read the great plays by the great writers (Chekhov, Williams, and O'Neill, to name a few), and you promise to read as much about the craft by the great teachers (Stanislavski, Hagen, Adler, and Meisner, to name a few). You must make a commitment to yourself that you will pursue this for as long as you possibly can and as long as it is fun and your desire for it does not wane. If you ever come to a point where it is no longer what you need in your life, then you graciously accept that fate. That is not a negative commentary on your ability; it is just the reality that many good, talented people must face from time to time. There is nothing wrong with that acceptance.

Entitled to Make a Living

As you keep your skill level new and fresh, you also accept the fact that you have a right to make a living by using your skills. Most people cannot make a living in the theatre, so if you don't come from money—and most of us don't—then you determine what your approach will be to achieving audition opportunities that will lead to paying jobs in television and film. It is hard to make a living as an artist, so one must take the art and try to make a living from it. Some actors do this in daytime television, others in primetime, some in films, and many successful actors through a combination of all.

The Television Audition Technique

I strongly urge you to believe in this television audition technique that I have developed and explained in this book. I have gotten a great amount of positive feedback from people who have tried it in their own pursuit of a career. I believe it sets up the actor to have a confident and successful audition. If you can buy into the philosophy, then you are even further along than most. If after the twenty-five auditions that you monitor in your workbook you determine this isn't for you, then so be it. You bought a book, read it, and gave it a try. My only concern for you is that you will revert back to what may not have been working for you previously. I encourage you to seek another technique and give that your best effort. In saying that, I am confident you will gain something from this book. The technique is the foundation for the work you do at home in your preparation time, but your own ability as an actor must complement your choices and the technique. Technique alone is not good enough. Talent alone is not good enough. The combination of the two empowers you for a future of confidence and success.

Look Yourself in the Mirror

One of the last bits of advice I can give you about being an actor in this industry is to encourage you to look yourself in the mirror. Not only at yourself, physically, on the outside, but internally, both spiritually and mentally.

Look at yourself and ask, "What kind of an actor am I?" This is a great question if you can answer it honestly. Every young actor wants to be the next Julia Roberts, or Tom Cruise, or Brad Pitt, but, for most, that will not be the case. Everyone wants to be the romantic leading man of a film or the guy that a sitcom is based around, but the truth is that someone has to play the best friend or the bad guy, or the plain-looking girl next door. The truth is, if you can look at yourself and accept the fact that you are the best friend, then you are on the business track to carving out a career. If you know that is your type, then you won't be asking your agent to get you in for the new series regular role on that primetime drama that everyone wants to audition for. Instead, you will hope for the chance to play that guy's buddy from college—the one fewer people might be auditioning for.

The Core Truth

All people have inside them what I like to call a "core truth." The core truth is the internal emotional connection you have to life. It is the morality that guides you through life. It is what dictates your own behavior. Some people are ambitious people by nature. Others are caring, and still others are mean. When I was a theatre director, I would instruct the ensemble to try to determine what the core truth of their character was. If you can get a grasp of the drive behind your characters, you will have a better understanding of why they behave they way they do.

To use this for audition purposes, you must try to determine what your own core truth is. If you analyze your own needs, desires, and behavior, you might be able to determine what is at your core. If you are able to determine it, then you should try to audition for characters that have the same, or at least similar, truths. The more you are like the character, the better chance you have of understanding that character. This does not mean that you shouldn't play roles that are dissimilar to your core, but in the early stages of your career, it is often an easier transition from yourself to your character if the role is closer to your own individual core truth.

My Casting Director Perspective

Please know that as a casting director, there is not a more exciting moment for me than watching an actor book a job. Sometimes this is when a young actor books his first speaking role on a show; for others, it is making it through the entire process, from first audition all the way through the screen test, and landing a coveted contract role. I love the moment when I get to inform the actor or the agent of this exciting news. What is even more exciting for me, in my job, is when I am handed a role to cast, and I know which actor I think is perfect for the role, and he actually gets the role and flourishes in it. There is no better feeling for me as a casting director. It confirms for me that I know what I am doing and looking for. This has happened several times to me. Many times, I do not know the actor when I start the process, but I meet him through the process. Still others I have known for years. Sometimes, an actor walks into the audition room for the first time and I get a sense that he could be the person; many times, if he shows that potential, he is on his way. Actors who I thought should have booked roles have done so, and sometimes actors who I think shouldn't actually do, too. When that is the case, I usually think there is a more appropriate role for that actor, but in the process, writers and producers may witness qualities in the actor that can take the character in a different direction than the original casting concept. Because of that, and because an actor got a role, I am equally happy for the actor, since I know how proud he feels about booking the job. It is a reward for many years of hard work, and for most, let's face it, a fulfillment of a dream. The point is that actors should know that casting directors want them to succeed. We are in your corner, and we are there for you.

Good Luck

Good luck to you and your pursuit of your acting endeavors. Keep the passion, don't lose your personality, and remember to have fun. Study and study and learn, and then condense it into your opportunity to audition. I think that wanting to be an actor is one of the most amazing, crazy, and courageous things one can do. You have an obligation to pursue it until you accept that it isn't for you. If you come to the realization that it is not for you, then look back and be proud of the effort that you made and the work that you did. If you are resilient and your career starts to roll, keep it rolling by being consistent with what got you to this level, and keep working hard to allow it to get you to the next level and beyond. Work very hard and put yourself in a position to get lucky. All the best to you as you practice and focus on the technique. Believe in it and it will reward you.

About the Author

Rob Decina is the Emmy-nominated casting director for the daytime drama *Guiding Light*. His other casting credits include the independent film, *A Tale of Two Pizzas*, and casting searches in New York for *Dawson's Creek*, *The Scorpion King*, and *National Lampoon's Van Wilder*. Before *Guiding Light*, he was the associate casting director at Warner Bros. Television in New York, where he was involved in the casting for *The West Wing*, *Third Watch*, and more than forty other primetime television pilots.

He has made television appearances on CBS's *The Early Show*, The Learning Channel, Bravo's *It Factor*, and SoapNet's *Soap Center*. He has been interviewed on the radio on the KTU 103.5 FM Morning Radio Show, as well as by many publications, including *Backstage*, *The Washington Times*, *Soap Opera Digest*, and *An Actor's Guide: Making It in New York City* by Glenn Alterman, to name a few.

He is the Artistic Director and Producer of the Young Connecticut Playwrights Festival and the Maxwell Anderson Playwrights Series, a yearly festival devoted to developing young playwrights.

Decina is an adjunct professor in communications at Pace University and has taught workshops and lectured at various colleges and theatre schools around the country, including Sarah Lawrence College, New York Stage and Film at Vassar College, the Neighborhood Playhouse, the Tepper Center for Careers in Theatre for Syracuse University, Miami University of Ohio, and Rutgers University. He teaches audition technique at TVI Studios in New York.

He has a Master's in Fine Arts in Theatre from Sarah Lawrence College and a Bachelor of Arts in Literature and Communications from Pace University.

He is a member of the Casting Society of America and has been nominated for two Artios Awards for Outstanding Achievement in Casting on a Daytime Episodic Drama. *The Art of Auditioning* is his first book.

Index

Books from Allworth Press

Allworth Press is an imprint of Allworth Communications, Inc. Selected titles are listed below.

Improv for Actors
by Dan Diggles (paperback, 6 × 9, 246 pages, $19.95)

Movement for Actors
edited by Nicole Potter (paperback, 6 × 9, 288 pages, $19.95)

Acting for Film
by Cathy Haase (paperback, 6 × 9, 224 pages, $19.95)

An Actor's Guide—Making It in New York City
by Glenn Alterman (paperback, 6 × 9, 288 pages, $19.95)

VO: Tales and Techniques of a Voice-Over Actor
by Harlan Hogan (paperback, 6 × 9, 256 pages, $19.95)

Career Solutions for Creative People
by Dr. Rhonda Ormont (paperback, 6 × 9, 320 pages, $19.95)

Promoting Your Acting Career
by Glenn Alterman (paperback, 6 × 9, 224 pages, $18.95)

Producing Your Own Showcase
by Paul Harris (paperback, 6 × 9, 240 pages, $18.95)

Creating Your Own Monologue
by Glenn Alterman (paperback, 6 × 9, 192 pages, $14.95)

Technical Film and TV for Nontechnical People
by Drew Campbell (paperback, 6 × 9, 256 pages, $19.95)

The Health and Safety Guide for Film, TV and Theater
by Monona Rossol (paperback, 6 × 9, 256 pages, $19.95)

Please write to request our free catalog. To order by credit card, call 1-800-491-2808 or send a check or money order to Allworth Press, 10 East 23rd Street, Suite 510, New York, NY 10010. Include $5 for shipping and handling for the first book ordered and $1 for each additional book. Ten dollars plus $1 for each additional book if ordering from Canada. New York State residents must add sales tax.

To see our complete catalog on the World Wide Web, or to order online, you can find us at
www.allworth.com.